School Learning
and
Cognitive Style

School Learning
and
Cognitive Style

Richard Riding

David Fulton Publishers
London

David Fulton Publishers Ltd
Ormond House, 26–27 Boswell Street, London WC1N 3JZ

www.fultonpublishers.co.uk

First published in Great Britain in 2002 by David Fulton Publishers

Note: The right of Richard Riding to be identified as the author of this work has been asserted by him in accordance with the Copyright, Designs and Patents Act 1988.

Copyright © Richard Riding 2002

British Library Cataloguing in Publication Data
A catalogue record for this book is available from the British Library

ISBN 1–85346–694–8

Typeset by FiSH Books, London
Printed in Great Britain by The Cromwell Press, Trowbridge, Wilts.

Contents

Preface

This book is based on the belief that it is the teachers who fundamentally make the school. Effective learning is a basic characteristic of a successful school. The key is not complex management systems, it is good quality teaching where staff have an enthusiasm for their subject and are effective in its delivery and have a concern for the pupils.

This book provides a simple approach to the use of teaching strategies to improve the quality of student learning and pupil care and management. It incorporates recent psychological developments on individual differences in learning. It is intended for both training and experienced teachers, since it offers new approaches in three key areas for effective learning: processing capacity; cognitive style; and understanding the structure of knowledge.

The first six chapters of the book provide a model of learning and detail the research evidence and the final chapters, 7 and 8, indicate practical applications.

I wish to thank Professor Eugene Sadler-Smith and Dr Hassan Dahraei for helpful comments on an earlier draft of the book.

Richard Riding
Birmingham, January 2002

Introduction and overview

Effective learning

The effectiveness of a school will depend on the quality of the learning that takes place. Potentially a lot of factors will influence this: the home background of the pupils, the prevailing peer culture, the ethos of the school, the quality of the school staff and the individual characteristics of the pupils. The first two of these, the home and the peer group, are generally beyond the control of the school. The last three can be changed or taken into account to dramatically improve learning and attainment.

A way of significantly raising teaching performance and consequently the efficiency of pupil learning is to improve the teaching strategies employed by the staff, and the learning strategies used by the pupils. This will have the dual effect of improving both staff job satisfaction and pupil self-esteem.

An effective approach will combine solid research findings with the experience, common sense and commitment on the part of the staff who implement it. This book aims to help a school to maximise its performance and to make the most of the potential of its students. It takes account of individual differences. Teachers have long recognised that pupils differ, but have lacked a clear means of taking account of such differences in their teaching.

The present approach focuses on the learning process and deals with the key elements of working memory, cognitive style and long-term memory. These are key to an understanding of individual differences. A schematic view of the information processing components of the learning process is shown below.

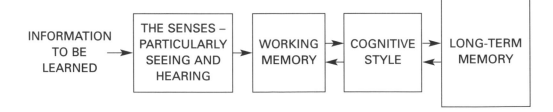

Information is received by the senses in terms of pictures and written words to the eyes and of sounds and speech to the ears. This information is then transferred to working memory.

- *Working memory* is where information is temporarily stored while we work out the meaning of what we see and hear, and long-term memory is where the analysed information is finally stored for future use. Working memory has a limited capacity whereas long-term memory has a very large capacity.
- The organisation and form of the information will be determined by the pupil's *cognitive style*. Cognitive style is an individual's preferred and habitual approach to organising and representing information.
- The meaning of information in working memory is determined in terms of the previously learned knowledge structure already in *long-term memory*. The information will then be linked to what is already known in the large capacity long-term memory.

There are three important educational implications of this information processing framework.

- With respect to working memory, while information is being received and analysed, it is very vulnerable to loss by displacement by the input of further information. As a pupil listens to the teacher, for instance, while he or she is analysing the sentence he or she has just heard, there is the danger that it may be displaced by the next sentence heard. Further, the individual will not be conscious of this loss, except that the partial information will not make sense. Pupils will differ in the effective capacity of working memory.
- Pupils learn best when the structure of the material and its mode of presentation matches their cognitive style.[1]
- Effective learning also requires that the pupil can link new information to what he or she already knows that is stored in long-term memory in order to give it meaning. If the relevant prior learning has not taken place then there will not be understanding.

The chapters that follow show teachers how they can develop the ways they teach, and improve their teaching strategies, to increase their effectiveness, and hence to establish a style-friendly teaching and learning approach. A teacher's own cognitive style will influence their teaching style. An awareness of individual differences in teaching and learning will help enhance learning and encourage positive pupil performance.

---

[1] Some writers use the term 'learning style'. Often, but not always, this corresponds to 'cognitive style'.

Some things are within the control of the teacher and can be changed, while others cannot. The focus will be on what the teacher can alter.

In outline the book comprises eight chapters. Chapter 1 puts school learning in context by considering the various factors that affect performance and identifying those that are within teacher control.

Chapters 1 to 6 describe the working components of the information processing system and the research evidence for them.

Finally, Chapters 7 and 8 consider a practical application of the research to school learning and behaviour management, and of the development of independent pupil learning and pupil learning strategies.

CHAPTER 1

Starting where you are

Chapter overview

Teachers will notice several behaviours related to learning. This chapter will consider the factors affecting school learning and behaviour. Some of these can be readily influenced by the school or the teacher, while other factors impact on learning but are largely beyond the control of the teacher.

Observable classroom behaviours

The teacher will observe a range of behaviours in pupils including:

- attainment;
- learning behaviour;
- conduct behaviour;
- emotional behaviour.

The factors affecting school performance

Four general areas will influence pupil performance:

- home background – parental care and recognition, parental control and educational background of the parents;
- peer influences – peer support, peer conformity and peer values;
- school – teacher care and recognition, teacher control and quality of teaching;
- individual characteristics – gender, working memory capacity, cognitive style, stability, prior knowledge and learning strategies.

What the teacher can affect

While home and peer influences are largely outside the control of the teacher, three key areas can greatly affect performance.

- By taking account of the individual characteristics of the pupils the teacher can adopt teaching strategies to facilitate learning.
- The effective management of behaviour will improve learning.
- Pupils can also be encouraged to develop strategies to maximise the effectiveness of their characteristics.

What the teacher sees – observable classroom behaviours

This consideration will begin with what is generally observable to the teacher in the school. Teachers will notice that some pupils appear more confident than others, that some behave in a cooperative way while others are disruptive, that some attend to the learning task while others are lacking in motivation or are poorly organised, and that some do well in assessments while others do not.

School attainment can be seen as part of a cycle in which four elements affect one another. The four elements are emotional behaviour, conduct behaviour, learning behaviour and attainment. Pupils' success at learning, as shown by their attainment, will influence their emotional behaviour and their motivation and conduct behaviour. The way pupils feel and behave, in turn, will determine the extent to which they attend to their work and hence influence their learning behaviour. The learning behaviour will then be related to their attainment. The elements of the cycle are shown in Figure 1.1.

Emotional behaviour

How a person feels about themselves will affect their performance. The level of emotional behaviour is likely to manifest itself positively in terms of such characteristics as a degree of self-assurance, a quiet self-confidence, an ease in associating with other pupils and adults, not appearing overly anxious or nervous, and not being unduly quiet or withdrawn.

The degree of emotional behaviour will reflect, on the one hand, the internal sources such as anxiety level and past experience, and on the other, the level of external stress which may come from the home, the school and the peers.

For rating by teachers, a general indication of self-perception of pupils may be obtained using the emotional behaviour items on the *Emotional and Behavioural Development Scale* (QCA 2000). However, an obvious problem with

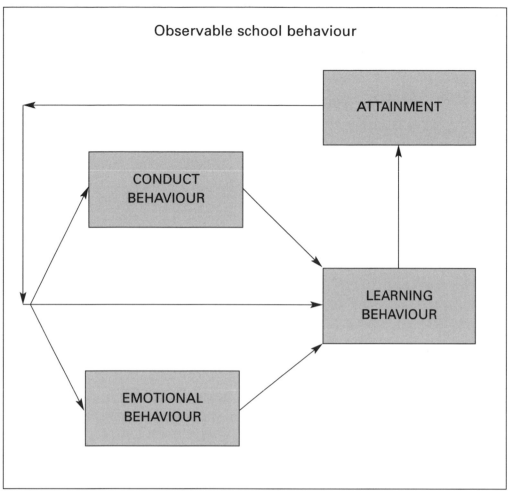

Figure 1.1 The school behavioural cycle

external assessment is that the observer cannot know exactly how a person feels.

Conduct behaviour

Teachers are likely to view conduct disorder as outward manifestations of misbehaviour such as verbal interruption, distracting other pupils, inappropriate moving about, and physical aggression to other pupils or the teacher. In the UK, the Elton Report (DES and Welsh Office 1989) suggested that teachers generally identify misbehaviour in these terms. Conduct disorder will usually result in reduced learning performance not only of the pupil who is misbehaving, but also of other pupils in the group who were distracted, since if pupils are not attending they will not be learning. By contrast, passive misbehaviour, such as inattention, 'daydreaming' and not completing work, is less likely to be seen as conduct disorder because it is not disruptive, but rather as 'learning disorder'. Girls generally display misbehaviour more passively in a manner that does not cause disruption; see, for instance, Schwartzman, Varlaan, Peters and Serbin (1995: 362–5). Passive misbehaviour, such as inattention and not completing work, was not likely to be counted since it was not disruptive. Conduct behaviour may be assessed by teachers using the conduct behaviour items on the *Emotional and Behavioural Development Scale* (QCA 2000).

Learning behaviour

Learning behaviour will include the extent to which an individual is attentive, has interest in learning, is well organised, shows perseverance, communicates effectively, works with others and seeks help as necessary. Learning behaviour may also be assessed using the learning behaviour items on the *Emotional and Behavioural Development Scale* (QCA 2000)

Attainment

Attainment will follow from the learning behaviour and will be the degree of learning that is usually manifested in terms of tests and examinations, but also in class exchanges and group work.

The factors affecting school performance

There are some things that are under the control of a class teacher and others that are not. It is useful to consider the overall picture and to recognise what teachers can change and what is largely beyond their control.

It may be noted that in the past there has been the tendency for researchers and practitioners to take a fairly narrow view and for their work to focus on one aspect to the exclusion of others. What is needed is to adopt an integrating approach, and to see the relative effects of the variables both singly and together.

The operation of the cycle

The behavioural cycle does not operate in isolation, nor in a completely sequential manner in terms of causation. Several more fundamental characteristics and experiences will also affect emotional, conduct and learning behaviour. Reviews of the possible contributory factors to problem behaviour have suggested a range of variables, including individual characteristics (e.g. impulsivity, intelligence), home background (family, socio-economic level) and peer influences (see, for instance, Charlton and George 1993), as summarised in Figure 1.2, which groups variables under the headings of the home background, the quality of schooling and the attitudes and values of the peers, and individual characteristics.

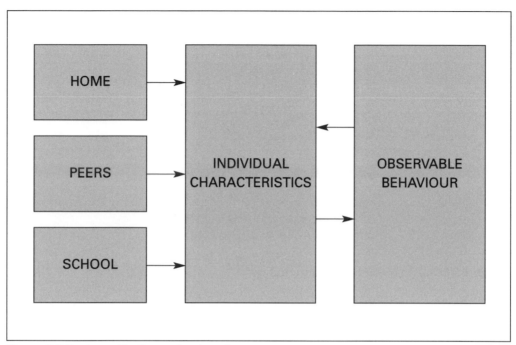

Figure 1.2 Factors affecting school performance

The variables that contribute to performance on the behavioural cycle will be examined in more detail. The characteristics will be considered from top to bottom and from left to right of Figure 1.2, and for each their individual effect on the observable behaviours will be noted. However, home, school, peers and the individual will all interact with one another in affecting the behavioural cycle.

Home background

Pupils will be influenced by their home background. There are three aspects of the home that are likely to impact on the child, and these are shown in Figure 1.3.

The features of an *ideal* home would include (1) a loving care and concern by the parents for the child and recognition for its achievement, (2) sensibly and lovingly applied control and discipline, and (3) the parents being of sufficient educational level and ability and having the willingness to provide an

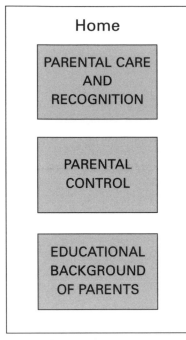

Figure 1.3 Features of the home background

interesting and stimulating environment and to provide learning resources in the home/family.

The opposite characteristics to the ideal would be parental neglect giving a feeling in the child of rejection, lack of control or repressive control, and educational impoverishment.

Home background and emotional behaviour

It may be assumed that love and recognition by the parents for the child are essential for the child's well-being. At the most basic level such care will result in the child's being adequately fed and clothed. Just as important for the child's happiness is the higher level of the love and recognition that is necessary to produce a feeling of security and self-worth in the child which will lead to self-assurance.

There is evidence that lack of love and recognition in childhood result in a feeling of insecurity, low self-worth and potentially of a difficulty in interpersonal relationships (e.g. Bowlby 1988). Research on the importance of attachment (e.g. Collins and Read 1990; Levy and Davis 1988; Pistole 1989) emphasises the importance of secure attachment for the development of the capacity for intimacy and relationship satisfaction that predisposes the ability to make and keep friends. Avoidant attachment is associated with lower levels of intimacy and emotional intensity, as well as lower levels of commitment and satisfaction. Loeber and Stouthamer-Loeber (1986), in considering the results of British, American and Scandinavian studies on family factors and behaviour, concluded that the primary influence was neglect of their children by parents, and the consequent lack of an active interest in them and a relationship with them. In a review, Mruk (1999: 72–4) found evidence that self-esteem is related to parental involvement, warmth, expectation, respect for the child and consistency of parenting.

Home background and conduct behaviour

It may be argued that consistent and reasonable control is important since it is necessary if the child is to internalise values and moral boundaries for behaviour. Without these the child will lack self-control and a view of acceptable behaviour. Control and discipline will need to be lovingly and sensibly applied by the parents. This is in contrast to harsh unfeeling discipline on the one hand, and a lack of control allied with spoiling on the other. The consequence of the levels of love and control are shown in Figure 1.4. Although only the extremes are shown, each will be a continuum.

		LOVE	
		ABSENT	PRESENT
CONTROL	ABSENT	Uncontrolled child	Spoilt child
	PRESENT	Fearful and restless child	Good internalisation of self-control

Figure 1.4 Parental love and control effects

Winkley (1996: 92), for instance, has argued that the main underlying cause of conduct disorder in the majority of instances is the lack of a stable and secure family relationship. A child's behaviour is likely to be greatly influenced by the quality of love and the stability of the home environment, and the control received (Charlton and George 1993: 32–6).

There is probably the need for a clear, consistent system of rules and control to be applied to children as they develop which is based on a loving relationship. If the control structure is not applied, or if control is applied in an unloving way, then an internalised self-control system will not be developed. Poor parental control has been found to be related to problem behaviour (e.g. McCord 1979; Wilson 1980; Riley and Shaw 1985).

There is evidence, then, that for a child to feel secure and self-controlled two elements are required: (1) the experience of love and recognition from the parent(s) to foster within the child an adequate level of security, self-esteem and self-worth; and (2) a reasonable, consistent and lovingly applied system of discipline and control, so that the child develops an internalised self-control. The absence of either or both of these elements is likely to result in problem behaviour being exhibited.

Home background and learning behaviour and attainment

Two aspects of the parents will affect learning behaviour and attainment – their commitment to their children and their learning resources.

In terms of commitment, for parents of a given intellectual level, the time and effort they spend encouraging and facilitating their children's learning activity will affect intellectual development. This will act by the parents helping their children to learn, for instance, language skills such as reading, and also incidentally by the parents sharing their own enthusiasm for learning and exploring new ideas and interests with their children.

With respect to learning resources, these will include both the intellectual level of the parents and the provision and appropriate use of learning media such as books, television and computer equipment, and access to educational software and the Internet.

Rumberger, Ghatak, Poulos, Ritter and Dornbusch (1990) found that dropping out of school was associated with parents being less involved in their children's education. Zimiles and Lee (1991) concluded that students from stepfamilies and single-parent families were almost three times as likely to drop out of school as their counterparts from intact families. Griffin and Morrison (1997) observed that the home literacy environment was a significant predictor of a child's achievement. Luster and McAdoo (1996) found that the mother's educational level and involvement in kindergarten was related to academic performance. Pong (1998) showed that family characteristics such as socio-economic status, having two parents, parents who discuss school matters with their children, all affect achievement. Downey (1995) investigated parental type as a resource and as a mediator between family structure and educational performance. It was found that step-parent households had less parental resources than in mother/father households, and resulted in lower educational outcomes.

Peer influences

Pupils are likely to be influenced by the attitudes and values of their peers (e.g. Brown, Eicher and Petrie 1986). A particular peer society in a school will often comprise several distinct groups and an individual pupil's membership of these will be influenced by home background. Durbin, Darling, Steinberg and Brown (1993) found that parenting styles labelled as authoritative, authoritarian, indulgent and uninvolved affected adolescents' orientation towards particular peer groups. Generally, the authoritative style orientated towards well-rounded groups that valued adult and peer-supported norms. Uninvolved parents tended to result in pupils who did not hold adult values, and indulgent parents led to pupils who wanted a 'fun culture'. The type of influence will depend on the peer culture and the difference between it and the culture of the school. This means that its effects are likely to be complicated. Where the school culture and the peer culture agree then they will tend to reinforce one another. The peer features are shown in Figure 1.5.

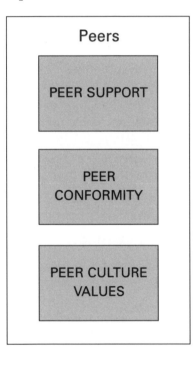

Figure 1.5 Peer features

The peer group and emotional behaviour

Peer groups will differ in the extent to which they are supportive. Further, peer recognition and support will derive from what the peer values accept. Pupils wanting support will need to conform to the peer values.

The peer group and conduct behaviour

The strength of the peer conformity will largely depend on the number of different peer groups available to the pupil. Where there is a uniform peer attitude its influence will be strong in the direction of the peer values. The extent of the influence is likely to interact with the individual's cognitive style and level of stability. Those of wholist cognitive style are more likely to conform to peer values than analytics. This is considered in Chapter 5.

The peer group and learning behaviour and attainment

In a middle-class school where the pupils accept the value of education and strive to do well in examinations, and the school also holds those values, then the pupils will be highly motivated to succeed. By contrast, in a school where the pupils consider education to be irrelevant then the mismatch with the school's values will result in pupils lacking motivation.

School

Rutter, Maughan, Mortimore and Ouston (1979) have drawn attention to the differences between schools in their effects on children's behaviour and attainment. There are three aspects of the school and the teachers within it that will affect pupils. The first is the extent to which the teachers show care and concern for the pupils and value them as individuals. The second is the control and discipline exercised by the teachers in setting clear and reasonable rules to provide clear boundaries for behaviour. Thirdly there is the quality of the teaching with regard to producing efficient and effective learning. These elements are summarised in Figure 1.6.

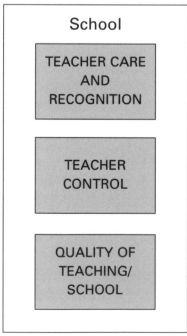

Figure 1.6 Features of the school

The school and emotional behaviour

Potentially, the school will have a profound effect upon the pupil's emotional behaviour. The *ethos* of the school will include the way in which pupils are viewed by the staff. Where a school values pupils as individuals and treats them with respect, this will affect the way pupils perceive themselves. The school should also avoid undue and unnecessary stress, particularly for more sensitive pupils.

The school and conduct behaviour

The school will have a significant influence upon conduct behaviour. The *rule system* of the school will include the structure of the school rules, their reasonableness and relevance, and their degree of enforcement and the clarity of boundaries they set. A further feature here is the extent to which teachers uniformly and fairly apply the rule system. Ogilvy (1994: 197) pointed out that in a school particular pupils may be disruptive only with certain teachers, and that pupil behaviour varies with context.

The school and learning behaviour and attainment

The school's impact on learning behaviour will be in terms of the extent to which the learning experience is made interesting and meaningful, and real active learning takes place. The quality of the teaching will be reflected in the degree to which the learning is meaningful and also the type and extent of learning strategy development that is available.

Meaningful learning depends upon pupils being able to relate the new information presented to what they already know (e.g. Ausubel 1968) and the teaching needs to structure learning to facilitate this, as described in Chapter 6.

Pupil strategy development requires a recognition of individual differences and of variation in style and intelligence, for instance, and that different pupils will learn best in different ways, and thus of the need for pupils to acquire learning strategies that make their learning more efficient (see Chapter 8).

Individual characteristics

The individual characteristics are of two types – those that are largely in-built and those that are learned and can be developed. As can be seen in Figure 1.7, the first category, shown within bold borders, will include gender, intelligence, degree of stability and cognitive style. The second comprises memories of experiences and prior learning knowledge, and learning strategies. The experiences will include the effects of parenting and peer influences and past learning experiences. The features of the individual are shown in Figure 1.7.

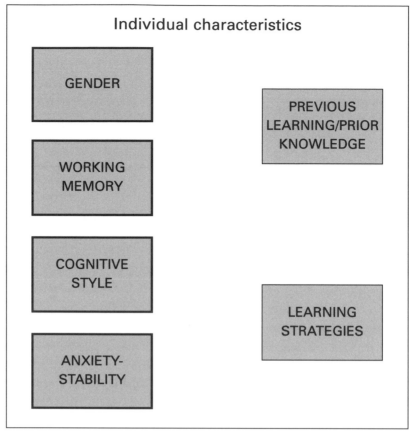

Figure 1.7 Individual characteristics

The features in the first category are more readily assessed in a general sense than those in the second. Measures exist of gender, working memory, cognitive style and anxiety-stability.

Changing the changeable – what the teacher can affect

There is usually little that the teacher or the school can do to change the home situation. To some extent it may influence the peer culture, but its main possibility will be in changing its own ethos and effectiveness, and this will be by taking account of the in-built characteristics of the pupil and of adapting learning to build a good structure of knowledge as a basis for future learning, and of facilitating the development of learning strategies to enable pupils to make the best of their capabilities and become independent learners.

The approach of this book is to recognise and understand the influences on pupil learning and behaviour and to take account of these and particularly to act on what the school and the teacher can change. While a sensitive and sensible management system in the school is important, the main effect will probably be due to individual teachers and their personal effectiveness and the Chapters 2 to 6 that follow will consider the possible ways in which the teacher can be more effective.

Four hindrances to learning will be considered:

- loss of information during learning because of slow processing causing an overflow in the information processing system;
- poor processing because of cognitive style mismatch;
- lack of understanding because of insufficient or poorly organised prior knowledge;
- poor conduct and emotional behaviour due to insufficient care and recognition, and a lack of clear rules and boundaries.

CHAPTER 2

Working memory and processing capacity

Chapter overview

This chapter will consider working memory capacity and its effect on learning.

Meaningful learning and working memory

- Pupils give new information meaning in terms of what they already know. Meaning is analysed in working memory.
- However, this has a limited capacity and information in it is vulnerable to loss if the system is overloaded.

Features of working memory

- The working memory system comprises three components: the central executive, and two slave systems – the phonological loop which stores verbal information and the visuospatial sketch pad. The central executive is responsible for control and integration of information from the phonological loop and visuospatial sketch pad.
- There are individual differences in the effective capacity of working memory. Individuals may differ in both the capacity they have available and the efficiency with which they use it.
- Working memory is also influenced by the level of the pupil's neuroticism-stability. Anxiety reduces the effectiveness of working memory.

Working memory assessment and learning performance

- Working memory capacity can be assessed by giving tasks that exceed its capacity and cause overflow and follow the pattern: present A – processing task – recall A.

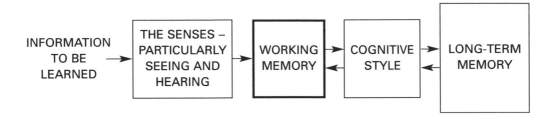

Meaningful learning and working memory

Ausubel (1968) has argued that in meaningful learning the new material is firstly given meaning in terms of what is already known, and is then incorporated into the organised structure of memory. This is in contrast to rote learning where the information is incompletely accommodated because the learner lacks the necessary related knowledge.

Examples of meaning

What the pupils currently know which is relevant and related to the present lesson is the most crucial determiner of whether learning will be meaningful. Since this is an important point, let us try a couple of simple examples. What do you make of the following words, 'dog', 'quagga'?

Take 'dog' first. You found this word very meaningful because it is well organised in your memory. It readily brought many associations. It may have evoked a mental picture; it has associations with similar concepts like fox, wolf and, perhaps, cat; it has associations with examples of the concept such as Alsatian, poodle, collie; it has associations with more inclusive ideas like animal and mammal. Thus 'dog' readily produces many associations, and it is this variety of associations that makes the word meaningful for us. If we were to read a story with a dog in the plot, we would experience no difficulty in understanding it.

By contrast, if the tale featured a quagga it is likely that things would be different, because for most readers the term lacks meaning. That is, when we read the word we get no associations and the word is nonsense, and so we cannot link new information to it.

What would make the term 'quagga' meaningful? Well, if you were told that a quagga was an animal related to the donkey and the zebra, and that quaggas are now extinct but once lived in southern Africa, then this would make the word mean something to you, because you would be able to relate, or link, it to concepts like 'donkey', 'zebra' and 'Africa', which are already familiar to you. Learning is like this. Pupils give new information meaning in terms of what they already know.

If the pupil is unable to relate the new information to what he or she already knows then it will be meaningless and probably not learned or at best learned in a rote manner, and learning is not part of a structure of information.

It follows from this that a crucial principle of successful teaching is that the teacher starts each topic from where the pupils are at in knowledge terms.

Working memory and long-term memory

In considering learning, it is useful to distinguish between *working memory* and *long-term memory*. The diagram above shows the path of information from the senses to long-term memory.

Information is received by the senses in terms of pictures and written words to the eyes and of sounds and speech to the ears. This information is then transferred to working memory. Working memory is where information is temporarily stored while we work out the meaning of what we see and hear, and long-term memory is where the analysed information is finally stored for future use. Working memory has a small and limited capacity whereas long-term memory has a very large capacity.

The meaning of information in working memory is determined in terms of what is already in long-term memory.

Working memory refers to the temporary storage of information which is necessary for performing cognitive tasks such as comprehension, reasoning and learning. Basically, new information is temporarily stored in working memory while its meaning is determined prior to its transfer to the more permanent long-term memory. A practical feature of working memory is its limited capacity and the vulnerability to loss of information from displacement by further incoming information. Thus the capacity of an individual's working memory is critical for effective learning.

The important educational implication is that while information is being received and analysed in working memory, it is very vulnerable to loss by displacement by the input of further information. As a pupil listens to the teacher, for instance, while he or she is analysing the sentence just heard, there is the danger that it may be displaced by the next sentence he or she hears. Further, the individual will not be conscious of this loss, except that the partial information will not make sense.

The features of working memory

The components of working memory

Research on working memory has been reviewed by Baddeley (1999; 2000). He concluded that the working memory system comprises three components: the central executive, and two slave systems – the phonological loop and the visuospatial sketch pad (Baddeley 1986; Baddeley and Hitch 1974). Information is processed by either, or both, the phonological loop or the visuospatial sketch pad. The central executive is responsible for control and integration of information from the phonological loop and visuospatial sketch pad.

The central executive
The central executive is considered to function as a control system. It is a limited capacity attentional system, responsible for coordinating the input and output of information to and from the subsidiary slave systems, and for selecting and operating control processes and strategies. In addition to this, the central executive, as an active cognitive mechanism, fulfils many different functions, such as 'the regulation of information flow within working memory, the retrieval of information from other memory system such as long-term memory, and the processing and storage of information' (Gathercole and Baddeley 1993: 4). The central executive is assisted by the operation of the two slave systems, the phonological loop and the visuospatial sketch pad.

The phonological loop
The articulatory or phonological loop is a slave system specialised for the storage of verbal information over short periods of time. According to Baddeley (1986; 1990a; Gathercole and Baddeley 1993), the phonological loop has a limited capacity and is assumed to comprise two components: (a) a temporary phonological store, which holds information in phonological form; and (b) an articulatory control process, which serves to maintain decaying representations in the phonological store. Therefore, when we attempt to remember a telephone number for a few seconds by muttering it to ourselves, it is the phonological store that we use. Or when we are preparing to speak aloud, the articulatory control organises information in a temporal and serial fashion, and it deals with verbal information in terms of its articulation.

Hulme and Mackenzie (1992) drew an analogy between the phonological loop and a tape loop of specific length which can hold a message that fits onto the length of the tape. Based on this analogy, the temporal duration of the message will determine whether it fits on the tape loop. If it is too long for the phonological loop's limited capacity, some of the message will be lost or have to be stored in the central executive. Further, with assumption that tape speed is constant, the number of items (words, digits) that can be fitted on the phonological loop depends on the time taken to articulate them.

It has been argued that the simple model of phonological loop can account for a range of factors that affect memory span in terms of phonological similarity, word length, articulatory suppression and irrelevant speech (e.g. Baddeley 1986; 1990b; Baddeley, Gathercole and Papagno 1998; Baddeley and Logie 1992; Gathercole and Baddeley 1993).

The visuospatial sketch pad

The third component of working memory system is the visuospatial sketch pad. It is 'a slave system specialised for the processing and storage of visual and spatial information, and of verbal material that is subsequently encoded in the form of imagery' (Gathercole and Baddeley 1993: 17). In some respects, the visuospatial sketch pad is similar to the phonological loop because it deals with more than one stimulus at a time and has the ability to rehearse information. Further, Baddeley (1990b: 109) stated that, like the phonological loop, 'it can be fed either directly through perception, in this case visual perception, or indirectly, in this case through the generation of a visual image'. However, the visuospatial sketch pad contains visual or spatial information rather than the phoneme information used by the phonological loop. Researchers have argued that the visual (the visual cache) and the spatial (the inner scribe) components of working memory are functionally separate systems (Baddeley 1990b; Baddeley and Logie 1992; Logie 1995). Accordingly, the visuo and spatial working memory is assumed to be a visual temporary store and a spatial temporary store.

Individual differences in working memory performance

The phonological loop and visuospatial sketch pad are maintenance systems controlled by the central executive, which is a flexible work space with limited capacity. The word 'capacity' is thought to be 'an energy source that some people have more of than other people have' (Just and Carpenter 1992: 124). For example, a person with a larger memory capacity for language comprehension may draw on a larger supply of resources.

Moreover, the central executive as a control and coordinating system is assumed to have processing as well as storing functions that compete for a limited capacity. Hence, more demanding processes consume more of the available capacity, decreasing the amount of additional information that can be stored and maintained in working memory. Consequently, when greater effort is required to process information, less capacity remains to store the products resulting from that processing. Thus, the information processing operation of working memory is limited in two ways: capacity and speed (e.g. Baddeley 1999).

Daneman and Carpenter (1980; 1983), for example, argued for the relationship between individual differences in working memory capacity and limitations in reading comprehension. They hypothesised that working memory is used to represent the strategies and skills used in a complex mental task such as reading, with the remaining capacity used to store the resulting products of the reading comprehension. They suggested that while information is being processed and the products of this processing stored, the two functions, processing and storage, would compete for the limited capacity available to working memory. They also argued that individual differences in reading comprehension are due to variability between readers in the efficiency of their processing.

Working memory and neuroticism-stability

A relationship between anxiety level and memory capacity has been observed by several researchers (e.g. Eysenck 1992; Calvo and Eysenck 1996; Elliman, Green, Rogers and Finch 1997; Hopko, Ashcraft and Gute 1998). The general view is that some of the capacity of working memory is devoted to the objects of anxiety, and this reduces the resources available for general processing.

If stress increases anxiety, which in turn reduces the effective working memory capacity, then there is the problem that this reduction causes misunderstanding, confusion and uncertainty when processing information. This may in turn cause further stress and hence increase anxiety. There will thus be the possibility of a cyclic effect.

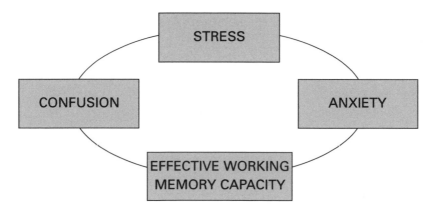

Figure 2.1 The stress cycle

In practical terms, if anxiety can be reduced then learning performance should increase.

Working memory assessment and learning performance

Assessment

Efforts have been made by several researchers to measure working memory capacity (e.g. Daneman and Carpenter 1980; Daneman and Tardif 1987; Turner and Engle 1989; Shah and Miyake 1996). Variations on the Daneman and Carpenter (1980) working memory span method have been widely used. An alternative approach is the Information Processing Index (Riding 2000a).

Working memory span

The Working Memory Span test (WMS) was devised by Daneman and Carpenter (1980) to measure working memory capacity. In this task, individuals are asked to read aloud or listen to a series of unrelated sentences of moderate complexity and then to do two things: (a) to comprehend each sentence; (b) to remember the last word of each sentence. The task typically starts with two sentences and increases to a point at which individuals are no longer able to recall all the terminal words. Reading span is then measured by the number of sentences in the largest set of sentences for which an individual is able to remember the last word of each sentence. According to Daneman and Carpenter (1980), this task is presumed to measure both processing and storage in working memory. This is in contrast to the Digit Span Test (digit span is assessed by a person listening to a string of digits, e.g. 92683715, and then recalling as many as they can), which measures only a storage component of working memory capacity. They found that the reading span task correlates highly with three different reading comprehension measures, namely answering fact questions, pronoun reference questions and the Verbal Scholastic Aptitude Test. Further, a listening version of the task also showed similar results to the reading version. Daneman and Carpenter (1980; 1983) argued that the rationale behind the Working Memory Span test was that the comprehension processes used in reading the sentences should consume less of the working memory resources of high span readers. These readers would thus have more capacity left to hold the final words of the sentences.

An alternative approach is the Information Processing Index (Riding 2000a). This computer-presented assessment shows railway trains comprising carriages of different colours entering the left side of a station into which the whole train disappears from view and then reappears on the right side with some carriage colours changed. Under the control of the person being assessed, the train enters the left side of the station where it is totally obscured from view and then emerges from the right side of the station one carriage at a time. The colours of some of the carriages are different from that on entry. Seven colours are used. The task is to indicate by pressing one of two marked keys, whether or not each carriage colour has changed. This is done as each carriage emerges from the station.

The assessee is able to view the train for as long as is wished before causing it to enter the station. While it is in the station and obscured from view the carriage colours have to be remembered. When the train is made to appear out of the station, a decision has to be made as to whether there is a carriage colour change. While this is being done, the information about the remaining carriages which are still obscured has to be retained in working memory. Except in the case when there is only one carriage, both retention and information processing are required. Both the amount to be retained and the quantity of processing increases with the length of the train. Thus the total number of carriages correctly identified is taken as the indication of effective working memory capacity. The score is the percentage of judgements that are correct.

Working memory and learning performance

Overall, there is substantial evidence that working memory capacity differs among individuals, and that this difference affects a wide range of cognitive tasks such as problem solving, reasoning, acquiring new vocabulary words, and reading comprehension (e.g. Cantor and Engle 1993; Conway and Engle 1994; Daneman and Carpenter 1980; 1983; Engle, Cantor and Carullo 1992).

However, as Baddeley (2000: 86–7) has noted, there is the possibility that apparent working memory capacity may actually reflect differences in the efficiency of processing strategies or skills rather than differences in working memory capacity, as such. In practice it appears likely that there are differences both in capacity and in skill efficiency.

The effect of effective working memory capacity on learning will be considered further in Chapter 4 in conjunction with cognitive style.

CHAPTER 3

Cognitive style

Chapter overview

This chapter will consider aspects related to cognitive style.

Cognitive style dimensions

- Cognitive style is an individual's preferred and habitual approach to organising and representing information. It has two dimensions: the wholist–analytic and the verbal–imagery.
- People differ in two basic ways: (a) whether they take a whole view or see things in parts – the wholist–analytic dimension; (b) whether they are outgoing and verbal, or more inward and often think in mental pictures or images – the verbal–imagery dimension.
- The style dimensions act in combination and individuals habitually use the most appropriate features of each of their styles in doing tasks.

The nature of cognitive style

Style needs to be seen within the context of other variables associated with personality and intelligence.
- The distinction between style and ability is that performance on all tasks will improve as ability increases, whereas the effect of style on performance for an individual will be either positive or negative depending on the nature of the task.
- Style is in-built, habitual in use and fairly fixed, while learning strategies may be developed by the pupil to help in situations where their style does not suit the task being done.

- Style appears to be distinctly different from other individual differences such as personality and gender.
- The origins of style may be where there are two competing ways of processing information and the individual uses the one of the pair that they are best at.

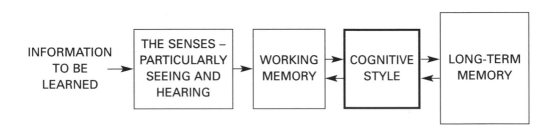

Cognitive style dimensions

Cognitive style is an individual's preferred and habitual approach to organising and representing information (Riding and Rayner 1998: 8). Cognitive style reflects the fundamental make-up of a person. It most probably has a physical basis. An individual will not really be very conscious of their style since they will have experienced no other.

Cognitive style affects the ways in which events and ideas are viewed. It therefore affects how a person may respond to, and think about, events in their life and make decisions. It also influences the attitudes they have to other people, and the ways they relate to them. An individual's style is the automatic way they respond to information and situations. It is constant for them and not something that appears to change. They cannot switch it on and off since it represents the way they are. However, when they are aware of their style they can develop strategies to utilise their strengths more effectively and to limit the effect of their weaknesses.

People differ in two basic ways:

- whether they take a whole view or see things in parts. We will call this way the wholist–analytic dimension;
- whether they are outgoing and verbal, or more inward and often think in mental pictures or images. This will be referred to as the verbal–imagery dimension.

The background to cognitive style has been reviewed by Riding and Cheema (1991), and Riding and Rayner (1998 Chapter 2), who concluded that the various style labels could be accommodated within two fundamental style dimensions, the wholist–analytic and the verbal–imagery. The dimensions may be summarised as follows.

- The *wholist–analytic* dimension of whether an individual tends to *organise* information in wholes or parts.
- The *verbal–imagery* dimension of whether an individual is inclined to *represent* information during thinking verbally or in mental pictures.

Each dimension represents a continuum, but for descriptive convenience may be divided into groupings, such as wholists and analytics (see Figure 3.1). The two basic dimensions may be assessed using the computer-presented *Cognitive Styles Analysis* (Riding 1991). The background to the development of the *Cognitive Styles Analysis* is provided in Riding and Cheema (1991) and a description of its construction is given in Riding and Rayner (1998: 44–6).

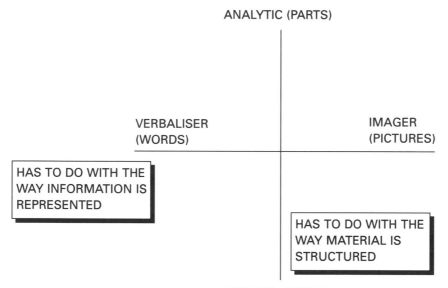

Figure 3.1 The cognitive style dimensions

These two styles are independent of one another. A person's position on one dimension of cognitive style does not affect their position on the other. However, the way they behave will be the result of the joint influence of both dimensions. We will now look at each style in turn and consider its effects on behaviour.

Wholist–analytic style

This dimension of style affects the way in which people think about, view and respond to information and situations. This will affect the way they learn and organise information, how they teach, and their relationship with colleagues and pupils.

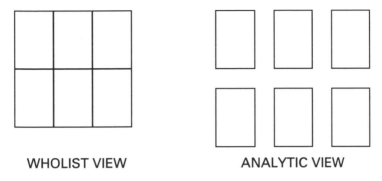

WHOLIST VIEW   ANALYTIC VIEW

Figure 3.2 Wholist and analytic views

Wholists tend to see a situation as a whole, and are able to have an overall perspective and to appreciate its total context. By contrast, analytics will see a situation as a collection of parts and will often focus on one or two aspects of the situation at a time to the exclusion of the others. Intermediates will be able to have a view between the extremes which should allow some of the advantages of both. Figure 3.2 shows in a schematic way how a situation or information might be perceived by wholists and analytics. The former view tends to be unified, and the latter more separated into parts.

For wholists, not only are the parts not separated, but there is possibly the danger that the distinction between them is blurred so that it is very difficult to distinguish the issues that make up the whole of a situation (see Figure 3.3).

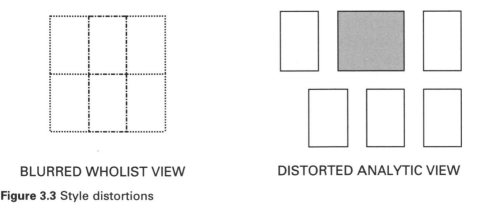

BLURRED WHOLIST VIEW   DISTORTED ANALYTIC VIEW

Figure 3.3 Style distortions

By contrast, the analytics will tend to focus on just one aspect of the whole at a time and this may have the effect of distorting or exaggerating it, or making it more prominent with respect to the rest, and so there is the possibility of getting it out of proportion to the total situation.

The positive strength of the wholists is that when considering information or a situation they see the whole 'picture'. They are 'big picture people'. Consequently they can have a balanced view, and can see situations in their overall context. This will make it less likely that they will have extreme views or attitudes. The negative aspect of the style is that they find difficulty in separating out a situation into its parts.

For the analytics, their positive ability is that they can analyse a situation into the parts, and this allows them to come quickly to the heart of any problem. They are good at seeing similarities and detecting differences. However, their negative aspect is that they may not be able to get a balanced view of the whole, and they may focus on one aspect of a situation to the exclusion of the others and enlarge it out of its proper proportion.

Intermediates will be between the positions of wholists and analytics.

Verbal–imagery style

This style has two fundamental effects that have implications for behaviour, teaching performance and relationships: the way information is represented, and the external/internal focus of attention.

Representation

It affects the characteristic mode in which people represent information during thinking: verbally or in images.

If a person reads a novel, for instance, they can represent the actions, happenings and scenes in terms of word associations or by constructing a mental picture of what they read. Just as we can set down our thoughts on paper in two possible ways, in words or in sketches, so we can also represent them in our minds in those two modes. We can think in words, or we can think in terms of mental pictures or images.

On this dimension people may be categorised as being of three types: verbalisers, bimodals or imagers.

- *Verbalisers* consider the information they read, see or listen to, in words or verbal associations.
- *Bimodals*, in the middle, tend to use either mode of representation.
- When *Imagers* read, listen to or consider information, they experience fluent, spontaneous and frequent mental pictures either of representations of the information itself or of associations with it.

All groups can use either mode of representation if they make the conscious choice, e.g. verbalisers can form images if they try, but it is not their normal, habitual mode.

The style thus affects the processing of information and the mode of representation and presentation that an individual will prefer, and this will affect the types of task they will find easy or difficult.

A practical implication is that verbalisers will often learn better by reading text, and imagers by looking at pictures.

External–internal focus

The second effect is that it influences the focus and type of an individual's activity – externally and stimulating in the case of verbalisers, and internally and more passive in terms of imagers. This has implications for social relationships, and also for the type of work and environment people will be content in.

For verbalisers, the focus will be outward to others and they will prefer a stimulating environment. They will see the social group as an extension of themselves and be socially aware. For imagers, the focus will be more inward, and they will be more passive and content with a more static environment. They will view the social group as more distant from themselves, and may be less socially aware.

The style dimensions in combination

To facilitate a consideration of the interaction between the style dimensions and learning, their possible effects in combination will be outlined. The style dimensions may complement one another, on the one hand, or intensify one another, on the other, depending on the combination of the dimensions.

Individuals will from time to time encounter tasks for which their style is not appropriate. In such cases, a strategy that appears to be employed by individuals is to use, where possible, the other dimension as an alternative (e.g. Riding and Sadler-Smith 1992: 336). For instance, if someone were an analytic-imager, since the analytic aspect of their style will not provide an overview of a situation, they could attempt to use the whole-view aspect of imagery to supply it. If another person were a wholist-verbaliser, then since the analytic facility is missing, they might use the 'analytic' property of verbalisation as a substitute.

It is possible to group the style types in terms of the degree to which an individual's position on the two dimensions complement one another or are unitary and consolidate one another. The style groups may be clustered on the basis of a combination of style dimensions offering complementary facilities in contrast to those that offer similar facilities. The wholist-verbalisers and the analytic-imagers have a *complementary* combination, such that the facilities of one dimension may supplement those of the other. By contrast, the wholist-imagers and analytic-verbalisers have a *unitary* combination, since neither of these has the opportunity to use the other style dimensions to supply the missing facility, but rather duplicates the facilities available. An extended consideration of the style dimensions in combination is given in Riding and Rayner (1998 Chapter 6).

The ordering may be done by starting with the wholist-imagers, who have a unitary combination, and progressing in step-wise manner to the wholist-verbalisers, who have the most complementary combination. The order is given by the numbers in Figure 3.4, with the most unitary having a very bold border to their boxes, through to the most complementary having a light broken border.

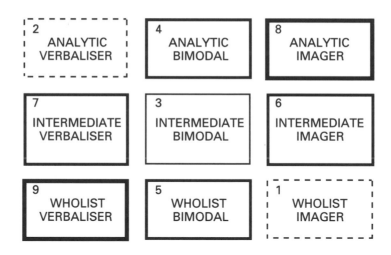

Figure 3.4 The cognitive style dimensions in combination

If these are then ordered from Complementary to Unitary they will be as follows.

UNITARY								COMPLEMENTARY
WI	AV	IB	AB	WB	II	IV	AI	WV

The nature of cognitive style

The distinction between style and ability

Cognitive style as assessed by the *Cognitive Styles Analysis* appears to be independent of intelligence (Riding and Pearson 1994; Riding and Agrell 1997). This is important since it helps to establish the distinction between style and ability, which has the requirement that style and ability be unrelated.

Carroll (1993: 554–60) considered a number of style measures and concluded that many of them were in reality aspects of ability. It will follow from this that for any measure of style to be valid, it must not also be a measure of ability. These two points will be considered.

What are the characteristics of style that distinguish it from ability? McKenna (1984: 593–4), in considering the nature of cognitive style as distinct from ability, highlighted four distinguishing characteristics.

- Ability is more concerned with level of performance, while style focuses on the manner of performance.
- Ability is unipolar while style is bipolar.
- Ability has values attached to it such that one end of an ability dimension is valued and the other is not, while for a style dimension neither end is considered better overall.
- Ability has a narrower range of application than style.

Both style and ability may affect performance on a given task. The basic distinction between them is that performance on all tasks will improve as ability increases, whereas the effect of style on performance for an individual will be either positive or negative depending on the nature of the task. It follows from this that for an individual at one end of a style dimension, a task of a type they find difficult will be found easier by someone at the other end of the dimension, and vice versa. For instance, if the dimension were the verbal–imagery style, then verbalisers would find pictorial tasks more difficult than would imagers, but they would find highly verbal tasks easier than would imagers. In other words, in terms of style a person is *both* good *and* poor at tasks depending on the nature of the task, while for intelligence, they are *either* good *or* poor.

It is in the nature of a style, as distinct from an ability, that it should interact with a variable such that the relative performance of an individual at one extreme of a dimension should be higher than that of a person at the other end in one condition, but that the situation should be reversed when the condition is changed. This is shown schematically in Figure 3.5.

Figure 3.5 shows an idealised relationship which in practice is not likely to be so linear and the crossover may not be at the centre of the dimension.

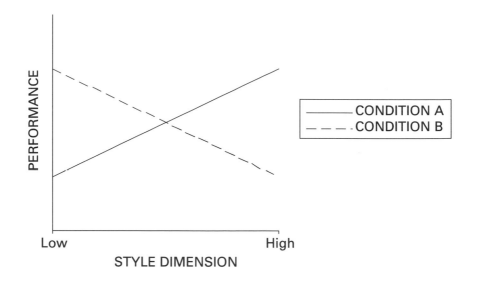

Figure 3.5 Schematic graph of performance and condition

Further, in many real-life tasks there is likely to be an interaction between the two dimensions and the condition, rather than an effect of only one of the dimensions without any effect of the other. However, single dimension interactions have been observed.

For the wholist–analytic dimension, this type of interaction was observed in the case of Douglas and Riding (1993) in a study on recall of the effect of the position of a prose passage title, and by Riding and Grimley (1999), who found that wholists learned better from computer-presented information and analytics from more traditional methods.

In the case of the verbal–imagery dimension, the interaction was found in the studies by Riding and Douglas (1993) on 'text-plus-text' versus 'text-plus-picture' presentation of learning material, and by Riding and Watts (1997) in the observed preference for verbal or pictorial formats of instructional material.

Cognitive styles versus learning strategies

It is useful to distinguish between *cognitive styles*, which are in-built, habitual in use and fairly fixed, and *learning strategies*, which may be developed by the pupil to help in situations where their style does not naturally fit the task being done. The development of learning strategies is considered in Chapter 8.

Style and other individual difference variables

Style appears to be distinctly different in nature from personality and gender.

Personality

Riding and Wigley (1997), in a study of college of further education students aged 17–18 years, used a range of questionnaire measures of personality and attitude, for comparison with cognitive style, and these included (a) EPQ-R Short Scale (Eysenck and Eysenck 1991) Extraversion, Neuroticism and Psychoticism; (b) IVE Questionnaire (Eysenck and Eysenck 1991) Impulsiveness, Venturesomeness and Empathy; and (c) State and Trait Anxiety Inventory (Spielberger 1977). A factor analysis gave four factors: anxiety, impulsiveness, empathy and style. No personality measure loaded beyond ±0.33 on style.

Gender

There do not appear to be overall gender differences with respect to cognitive style. Differences are usually small and non-significant on both dimensions ($P<0.05$) (e.g. Riding, Burton, Rees and Sharratt 1995).

The origins of style

An obvious question concerns the origins of style. Style either is inbuilt or develops with experience. It could be that an individual is born with a predisposition to use one mode of representation in preference to another. If style is inbuilt, what is the mechanism of transmission? Are there style genes?

Whatever the mechanism, style appears to be present at a relatively early age. Riding and Taylor (1976) found that the verbal–imagery style dimension was strongly in evidence in 7-year-olds.

It may be that a style emerges from a difference between two complementary abilities. In order to illustrate this, if one deliberately over-simplifies how the brain works and considers that within it there is one processor for verbal information and another for pictorial, then supposing that, in an individual, these two processors have unequal speed and processing capacity, the individual will tend to use the one in preference to the other whenever possible, and this will lead to the establishment of a style, or habitual preference for one over the other.

Gardner (1983), among others, has argued that intelligence has a multiple basis in that there are a number of basic abilities. These basic abilities may include:

- working memory capacity
- reasoning ability

- verbalisation/verbal fluency
- imagination/imagery fluency

- whole view ability
- analytic view ability

- mathematical ability
- musical ability
- psycho-motor ability.

Style may then be a comparison of 'competing' abilities which can be used to do the same task. Style may develop early in life as people get into the way of preferring to use their better ability of a pair. Such competing ability pairs will include:

- verbalisation/verbal fluency and imagination/imagery fluency;
- whole view ability and analytic view ability.

CHAPTER 4

Cognitive style and learning

Chapter overview

This chapter will consider the effect of cognitive style on learning.

Style and learning performance

- The structure of the material to be learned interacts particularly with the wholist–analytic style dimension.
- With presentation mode the verbal–imagery dimension is important. Imagers tend to learn better from pictorial presentations than verbalisers, while verbalisers learn better from verbal presentations than imagers.
- For content type, individuals appear to learn best when the information can be readily translated into their preferred verbal–imagery mode of representation.

Learning and representational preferences

- Given a choice, verbalisers prefer text while imagers are attracted to material that contains illustrations. In doing work, imagers tend to use pictures, and verbalisers tend to use writing.

Working memory capacity, cognitive style and learning

- Working memory capacity has little effect for wholists but a large effect for analytics.
- Verbalisers are more affected by working memory capacity than are imagers.

Since the two fundamental cognitive style dimensions are likely to affect the structure of an individual's thinking and the forms in which information can be represented by a person, style has potential implications for learning performance. This chapter will consider the research evidence.

Style and learning performance

The learning performance of an individual is likely to be affected by an interaction between cognitive style and:

- the way the instructional material is structured;
- its mode of presentation;
- its type of content.

The structure of the material

The material to be learned may be considered to have structure in terms of both its external format and also its internal conceptual form and content. *Format structure* refers to the external appearance and physical arrangement of the presentation of the information. Included within format structure are such features as the position of titles, how the text is divided into paragraphs, sub-headings, and also the size of the display, or 'viewing window' – large spread versus small – which affects how much can be seen at a glance.

There is also the question of whether the information is presented in large chunks or in smaller steps. With the latter the student is guided through the information more closely than in the former.

In terms of *conceptual structure*, all information has a potential for being structured. This may be in terms of a logical sequence of the ideas or concepts it contains, or a serial, temporal order of the events it describes. However, there are often different ways in which the material can be arranged for the same topic.

A related aspect of structure is whether there is an *organiser* before the main presentation of the material to provide the student with a structural framework on which to hang the material. This would also supply a context for the interpretation of the information. In addition to or instead of this, there could be an overview at the end to provide a summary of the whole.

Several studies have found that an individual's position on the wholist–analytic dimension interacts with the structure of the learning material to affect performance.

Large step versus small step and overview

Riding and Sadler-Smith (1992) compared performance on three differently structured versions of computer-presented instructional material on central heating systems with 14–19-year-old students. The three versions presented that same information about five topics.

- *Version L* had large steps and consisted of relatively large chunks of verbal information with simple line diagrams.
- *Version O* comprised small steps of verbal information interspersed with pictorial or diagrammatic content, plus overviews at the start, before and after each topic and at the end.
- *Version S* was as Version O with small steps but minus the overviews.

There was a total of 17 recall test questions and the time taken to work through the material ranged from 16.5 minutes to 47.2 minutes, with a mean of 27.18 minutes. The recall efficiency in terms of the percentage correct recall per hour was used as an index of learning performance and this is given in Figure 4.1.[2] The four styles are grouped as unitary (wholist-imager and analytic-verbaliser) and complementary (wholist-verbaliser and analytic-imager).[3]

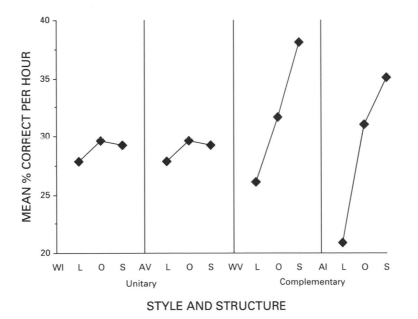

Figure 4.1 Learning efficiency, structure and cognitive style

---

[2] Adapted from Riding and Sadler-Smith (1992).
[3] This method of grouping styles was introduced in Chapter 3.

Inspection of Figure 4.1 indicates that for the two unitary groups, the structure had relatively little effect, with the groups performing in an 'average' manner irrespective of the format. For the complementary style groups, different ways of structuring the material had quite a large effect on performance, with the small-step format being most effective.

The wholist-verbalisers and the analytic-imagers did least well on the large-step format, but improved greatly with the overview-plus-small-step format. With the small-step version minus the overview they did even better. This was probably because the small-step format enabled them to analyse the information into its structure and to build up a whole view of it for themselves. The additional material in the form of summaries was therefore redundant and depressed performance, such that when it was not present, as in the case of just the small-step format, performance was considerably further improved.

By contrast, the analytic-verbalisers, who were good at analysing but not at having a whole view, and the wholist-imagers, who were the reverse, did better than the complementary groups on the large-step format, probably for different reasons: the former being very able to undertake their own analysis, the latter obtaining a whole view of the material without additional help. Consequently, neither the overviews nor the small steps improved performance very much, perhaps because they were constrained by their rather restricted methods of representing and structuring. Further work is necessary to find effective methods of helping these groups. It should be noted that gender was not included as a variable in this study.

Size of viewing window

Riding and Grimley (1999) with 11-year-old pupils compared learning from computer-presented CD-ROM multimedia instructional materials on science topics with performance from traditional methods as indicated by the results of Standard Assessment Tests (SATs) in science. The measure of performance in traditional work was taken as the total raw score on the two SATs for science, since this content appeared to be similar to that of the multimedia material. The overall multimedia performance was taken as the mean of the performance on 57 questions based on the information presented.

There was a significant interaction between wholist–analytic style and medium of presentation in their effect on recall. The wholists did better on the computer-presented material than on the traditional work while the reverse applied to the analytics. When compared to the traditional work attainment for the analytics, their lower multimedia performance may in part reflect the fact that the computer has a limited window of viewing and this reduces the performance of the analytics who find it more difficult to obtain a whole view, but does not adversely affect wholists.

Analytics tend to see material in parts and the restricted 'viewing window' which computer presentation affords can exacerbate this tendency. When using a computer to produce large word-processed documents, they may prefer to produce hard copies of it so that they can scan the pages to obtain a feel for the overall structure. Wholists are less likely to need to do this, since they naturally appreciate the whole.

Position of title

When presented with a prose passage for recall, Douglas and Riding (1993) found that with 11-year-old pupils, wholists did best when the title of the passage was given before the passage was presented, rather than at the end, although this had little effect for intermediates and analytics. The result was interpreted as due to the wholists, who were less able to impose their own structure on material, being helped by a title at the beginning to give some organisation to the material. Gender was not included as a variable in this study.

Presence of headings

Riding and Al-Sanabani (1998), with 10–15-year-old pupils attending a Yemeni school in the UK, studied the effect on reading comprehension (as indicated by recall performance) of dividing a one-page textual narrative describing the visit of an old friend into three paragraphs, each with a sub-heading. They found that this improved recall performance and that the degree of the facilitating effect was affected by the wholist–analytic style and gender of the student.

For wholists there was a similar improvement with the addition of format structure by both males and females, while for the analytics the males improved much more than the females. It may be that female analytics prefer to impose their own structure and find externally imposed structure less helpful than do males. Certainly the analytic females did well without the external structure. Similar effects were found for conditions where a summary was added.

Integration of information

Riding and Grimley (2001) found with 11-year-old pupils that with the source of information in text mode, the patterns for the males and females were similar. With the information available from text and pictures, the males improved in performance from wholist through to analytic, while the females declined with the worst performance by the analytics. It may be that the need to integrate the parts of the pictorial and the textual information is more difficult for the male wholists and the female analytics. This may have been particularly so since the pictures were in the form of cartoons and their content was by way of comical analogy from which deductions had to be made, rather than a simple presentation of information in a literal form.

This result accords with that of Riding and Read (1996), who, with 12-year-old pupils, found male wholists and female analytics to be more comfortable in situations that were closed and did not require divergent thinking.

Conclusion about structure

There is evidence that the structure of the material to be learned interacts particularly with the wholist–analytic style dimension. Basically, the findings appear to be as follows.

- Individuals of complementary style (wholist-verbalisers and analytic-imagers) are affected by the step size of the learning material and improve from large to small steps, while those of unitary style are not affected.
- Analytics need a large 'viewing window' compared to wholists, when dealing with information.
- There is an interaction between gender and wholist–analytic style in the facilitating effect of structure in the form of both headings and overviews, such that these most help male analytics and female wholists. By contrast, male wholists and female analytics are more comfortable in situations that are closed and predictable and do not require divergent thinking.

Having established that style interacts with structure in its effects on learning performance, further work needs to be done to investigate other aspects of conceptual structure that may have a bearing on practical learning effectiveness. For example, learning can proceed from the parts to the whole or from the whole to the parts. If one were teaching about how a telescope works, the *parts to whole* method would begin with the refraction, or bending, of light which passes through materials such as glass and plastic, on to lenses and magnification, and then to lenses combined together in a tube to make a telescope. The *whole to parts* method would be the reverse of this, and would start with the telescope and its practical use, and then would question how it works by taking it apart and examining the lenses and their arrangement, and then examining the action of light through the lenses, and so on to refraction.

Mode of presentation

There is a range of verbal, pictorial and auditory modes available for the presentation of information. It can be spoken, read, obtained from illustrations or from a combination of these. Since different styles have preferences for particular types of representation, they are likely to find particular media easier to learn from than others.

Text versus picture

Riding and Ashmore (1980) compared two modes of presentation (the textual and the pictorial) in a study with 11-year-old pupils. These presented groups of verbalisers and imagers (as assessed by the earlier *Verbal–Imagery Code Test*) with either a textual or a pictorial version of the same information. They found that verbalisers were superior with the verbal version and imagers when learning in the pictorial mode. Within the instructional context, while purely verbal presentation is often possible, an alternative entirely pictorial version without any text is rarely an option, as some words will also be necessary. However, it will usually be feasible to present information in both modes to some extent.

Text-plus-text versus text-plus-picture

Riding and Douglas (1993), with 15–16-year-old students, found that the computer-presentation of material on motor car braking systems in a text-plus-picture format facilitated the learning by imagers, compared to the same content in a text-plus-text version as shown in Figure 4.2.[4]

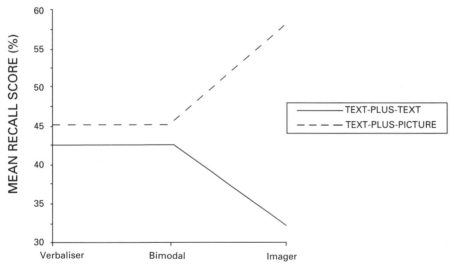

Figure 4.2 Recall and mode of presentation

---

[4] Adapted from Riding and Douglas (1993).

Further, the extent of the improvement was substantial for the imagers, approaching a doubling of their score. With the verbalisers, both modes resulted in similar learning. Gender was not a variable in this study.

Multimedia presentations

Riding and Grimley (1999), with 11-year-old pupils, considered learning from CD-ROM multimedia instructional materials on science topics. Three CD-ROMs were used with content on 'Gravity and Motion', the 'Geography of New Zealand', and the 'Natural History of Reptiles'. A pool of 57 recall test questions (16 about gravity and motion, 18 about New Zealand and 23 about reptiles) was constructed to reflect the types of presentation and content of the instructional material. They were analysed in terms of the mode of presentation of the information on which they were based into picture-plus-sound (PS), picture-plus-text (PT) and picture-plus-text-plus-sound (PTS). There was a significant interaction between wholist–analytic style, verbal–imagery style, gender and mode of presentation, and this is shown in Figure 4.3 for the complementary and unitary style groups.

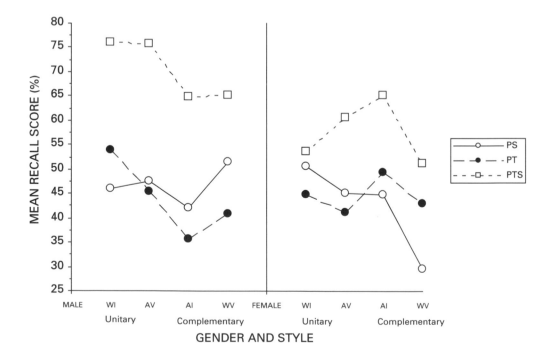

Figure 4.3 Recall, mode of presentation and style

Inspection of Figure 4.3 indicates that, overall, PTS is superior to PS and PT. The most likely reason for this is that with PTS the wider range of methods of presentation mean that there are more options for the individual learner to choose from, and consequently this meets the needs of a wider variety of styles, and results in better learning by more pupils.

Gender differences were observed for PS and PT in which there was a *reversal* with gender which was related to whether the styles were complementary, as with wholist-verbaliser and analytic-imager, or unitary, as with analytic-verbaliser and wholist-imager. PS involves two modes and two senses, 'look and listen' (two channels), while PT was two modes but 'look' only (a single channel). For the wholist-verbalisers and analytic-imagers (the complementary groups), males did better on PS than on PT, while this was reversed for females. For the unitary groups, the wholist-imagers and analytic-verbalisers, the tendency was the other way round with the male wholist-imagers better on PT, and the females on PS.

Basically, with males, complementary groups were best on a *separation* of the channels of pictures and words received aurally, while the females were best on the *single channel* of picture and words. With the unitary groups, the males were best on a single channel, while the females were superior on separate channels. With PS and PT the effects were perhaps due to differences in gender susceptibility to interference between competing modes of representation and/or channels of input.

Mode conclusions

Generally, imagers learn better from pictorial presentations than verbalisers, while verbalisers learn better from verbal presentations than imagers. It is also likely that lecturers and teachers will reflect their own style in the ways in which they present information, such that, for instance, verbalisers will use a highly verbal mode, while imagers will use pictures and diagrams to illustrate their words.

As with the wholist–analytic dimension, there was a gender interaction with the verbal–imagery dimension. The precise reasons for these are not clear and gender differences in information processing deserve considerably more research than they have received.

Type of verbal content

This section will consider the effect on performance of the type of verbal content of material to be learned. The section will begin with reading performance which is verbal in nature. It is also possible to discriminate between types of verbal material in terms of whether the content lends itself to the generation of images or is more abstract.

Reading performance

Initial reading performance, which is obviously a highly verbal task, has been found to be superior in verbalisers. Riding and Anstey (1982), with 7-year-old children, assessed reading accuracy and comprehension and found that both declined from verbaliser to imager, as assessed by the *Verbal–Imagery Code Test*. Riding and Mathias (1991), with 11-year-olds, observed that for reading accuracy this effect was still very pronounced for wholists, where wholist-verbalisers showed much greater proficiency at reading compared to wholist-imagers.

Concrete versus abstract content

In the case of the type of content of learning material, studies of 7, 11 and 12-year-old pupils indicated that imagers recall concrete, highly visually descriptive text better than more abstract, acoustically complex and unfamiliar text, while the reverse holds for verbalisers (Riding and Taylor 1976; Riding and Dyer 1980; Riding and Calvey 1981).

Riding and Calvey asked 11-year-old children to listen to tape recordings of four prose passages and after each passage to complete a recall test. The prose passages were selected to range on a continuum from highly visually descriptive and capable of being imagined, through to a high level of acoustic and semantic complexity with unfamiliar names and few visual details. Position of the verbal–imagery dimension was assessed by means of the *Verbal–Imagery Code Test*. Recall for the two extreme passages is shown in Figure 4.4.[5]

Inspection of Figure 4.4 shows that recall performance of the semantically complex content decreases from verbaliser to imager and for the visually descriptive material it increases.

Conclusion

In terms of content type, individuals appear to learn best when information can be readily translated into their preferred verbal–imagery mode of representation. It is of interest to note that not only the mode of presentation, but also the content itself, affects learning performance to an extent that is of practical significance.

---

[5] Adapted from Riding and Calvey (1981).

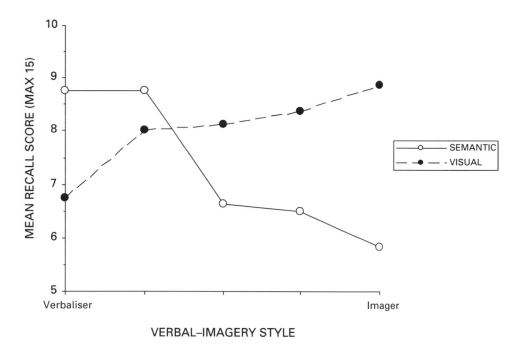

Figure 4.4 Recall of content type and verbal–imagery style

Learning and representational preferences

If people's preferences are in accordance with actual performance differences reported in the previous section, then it shows a consistency and persuasiveness about style. Further, as will be discussed in Chapter 8, preferences are an important part of strategy development.

Learning preferences

Format preferences

In a study by Riding and Watts (1997), female 16-year-old pupils were told within their class groups that three versions of a sheet giving information on study skills had been prepared for them, and that each sheet contained the same information but that the formats were different. They were then invited to come one at a time to the front of the class and to take one of the versions from the teacher's desk. Their choices were noted by the teacher. The versions were unstructured-verbal (paragraphs, without headings), structured-verbal (paragraphs, each with a clear heading) and structured-pictorial (paragraphs, each with a clear heading, plus a pictorial icon depicting the activity placed in the left margin). No pupils chose the unstructured-verbal version. With the two structured versions, there was a significant interaction with verbal–imagery style, with the majority of the verbalisers selecting the 'verbal' version and most of the imagers the 'pictorial' as shown in Figure 4.5.[6]

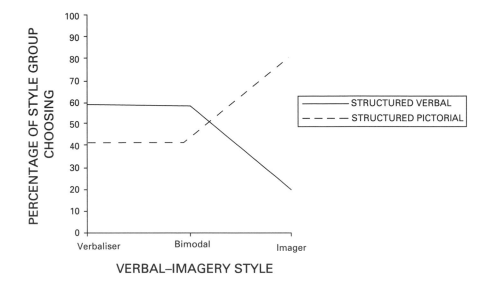

Figure 4.5 Verbal–imagery style and percentage choosing version

There was a lesser but still significant effect on the wholist–analytic dimension: the pictorial version was more attractive to the wholists, perhaps because it looked more 'lively', while with the analytics there was a slight preference for the more 'neat and tidy' verbal format. The results suggested that pupils are attracted to, and prefer to select, materials that appear to suit their own style.

Representational control and representation preferences

Voluntary and involuntary control

Riding and Dyer (1980: 278–9) distinguished between two levels of control of verbal and imagery performance: voluntary and involuntary. They suggested that in the former the individual makes a deliberate and conscious decision to generate an image or verbal response, while in the latter the image or verbal

---

[6] Adapted from Riding and Watts (1997).

representation occurs spontaneously without conscious effort. In the present context it may be argued that verbalisers do not use images greatly during involuntary information processing, although they can generate them successfully by conscious effort.

By contrast, imagers habitually use involuntary imagery as a means of representing information. Further, for imagers, mental pictures are likely to be less stable than those produced by verbalisers since they will be liable to interference and displacement by further involuntary intrusive images. It may follow that the converse applies to verbalisers and imagers with respect to verbal associations, and that verbalisers find that verbal associations tend to be less stable for them than they would be when consciously evoked by imagers.

Style and drawing from sight and memory

Douglas and Riding (1994) studied drawing performance with 11-year-old pupils. The pupils were asked to draw two pictures, one from memory and one from a picture. Judges rated the drawings of the verbalisers as significantly better than those of the imagers. It may be that the fluid mental pictures of the imagers interfered with the external representations.

Representational preferences

In an investigation by Riding and Read (1996), 12-year-old pupils were individually questioned about their preferences in the subjects of English language and science with respect to mode of working and social context. With respect to mode of working, in the case of the higher ability pupils, imagers – particularly wholists – reported that they used less writing and more pictures than verbalisers, especially where the subject allowed, as in science. The tendency by imagers to report the use of pictures, and verbalisers writing, increased with ability. There was evidence that lower ability pupils were more constrained by the usual format of the subject than were those of higher ability.

Riding and Douglas (1993), with 15–16-year-old students, studied the computer-presentation of material on motor car braking systems. A text-plus-picture format facilitated the learning by imagers, compared to the same content in a text-plus-text version. They found that at recall in the text-plus-picture condition, 50 per cent of the imagers used illustrations as part of their answers compared to only 12 per cent of the verbalisers. In other words, there are differences between the styles in the preferred mode of representing information.

It may well follow from this that in the case of individuals of the same ability and similar on the wholist–analytic dimension, the verbalisers are superior in speech, which benefits from involuntary verbal fluency, and relatively inferior in writing, where the lack of verbal control due to spontaneous involuntary verbal associations may be a hindrance. By contrast, imagers may be superior in written mode but inferior in the spoken mode.

Extending this notion to include the wholist–analytic dimension, it may be that the style groups will have most preferred and least preferred modes of expression. Common modes of expression are writing, drawing diagrams, drawing pictures and speaking, and the possible preferences are shown in Figure 4.6 by means of the numbers in brackets after each to denote first, second and third preferences.

Figure 4.6 shows that each of the four style groups have possible different basic preference for expression, and the further a group is away from the one that has the first preference, the lower their preference for that mode. Each group also has a least preferred mode. This arrangement is the probable one, and a systematic investigation of preferences is required.

Text (1) Speech (2) Diagrams (2) Picture (3)	ANALYTIC VERBALISER	ANALYTIC IMAGER	Diagrams (1) Picture (2) Text (2) Speech (3)
Speech (1) Text (2) Picture (2) Diagrams (3)	WHOLIST VERBALISER	WHOLIST IMAGER	Picture (1) Diagrams (2) Speech (2) Text (3)

Figure 4.6 Possible preferred modes of expression

Control and content

Sadler-Smith and Riding (1999) used a questionnaire approach to study instructional preferences in university business studies students. In terms of locus of control, the analytics preferred to have control themselves rather than to be controlled, while the wholists had no preference.

Riding and Staley (1998) gave a questionnaire to university business studies students which assessed their preferences about the content and presentation of their courses. For analysis the courses were grouped as information technology, accounting (Accountancy and Quantitative Methods, since both of these involved largely numerical concepts and computation), and management

(Organisational Behaviour and Business Workshop, both of which were concerned with the running of organisations). On the wholist–analytic dimension, intermediates were least happy with accounting and information technology and most happy with management. for accountancy and information technology, in terms of being positive about the courses, having a clear overview of the courses, least needing content overviews, finding the presentation order logical and liking the tutor's style, wholists were highest in their ratings, followed by the analytics, with the intermediates having the lowest ratings. Accounting and information technology require both a capacity for an overall view of the processes and their purposes, and the methodological following of rules. Wholists fit the first requirement and analytics the latter. Intermediates tend to *alternate* between both, which is useful for a more creative approach, but does not *consistently* give either.

With management, it was intermediates who were most positive, who generally found the presentation order logical and who most liked the tutor's style. Wholists in particular rated these less highly. Management requires a more creative approach, involving more problem-solving activities, which suits the intermediates more than the wholists.

With respect to the wholist–analytic dimension, when performance was considered it was noted that individuals underestimated their performance on the subjects that did not suit their style and overestimated it on those that did.

Representational and preference conclusions
Given a choice, imagers are attracted to materials that contain illustrations while verbalisers prefer text.

In doing work, the tendency by imagers to the use of pictures, and verbalisers writing, increases with ability.

Verbalisers can control images better than imagers, who in turn can control verbal associations better.

Working memory capacity, cognitive style and learning

Riding, Grimley, Dahraei and Banner (2001) with 13-year-old pupils investigated the effect of the effective capacity of working memory as indicated by the *Information Processing Index* (Riding 2000a) and style on overall learning behaviour as rated by the pupils' tutors. Learning behaviour was found to be affected by both working memory capacity and cognitive style in interaction. That is, one style was affected more by memory capacity than the other. The two style dimensions, wholist–analytic and verbal–imagery, will be taken in turn.

Wholist–analytic style, memory and learning behaviour

For the wholist–analytic dimension of style, the effect of working memory capacity on wholists and analytics is shown in Figure 4.7.

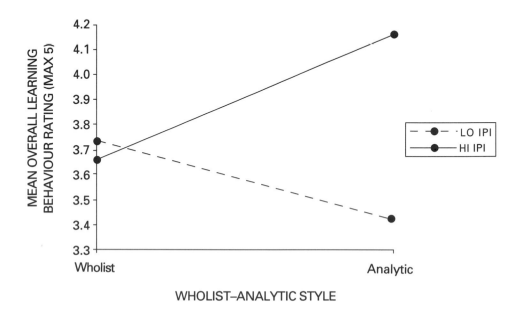

Figure 4.7 Learning behaviour memory and wholist–analytic style

Inspection of Figure 4.7 shows that working memory capacity has little effect for wholists but a large effect for analytics. This is reasonable since analytics are likely to have an elaborated approach to processing information which would involve examining all aspects and considering the full range of options. Such an approach is likely to result in good performance, but to be successful requires the availability of sufficient processing capacity. Consequently, when capacity is low, the analytics are unable to complete the processing and performance is depressed. However, when memory capacity is high, it is possible to complete the elaborated processing with resulting superior performance. The wholist approach requires less processing capacity and presumably memory capacity is in most cases sufficient, and this approach results in average performance irrespective of memory capacity.

Verbal–imagery style, memory and learning behaviour

Figure 4.8 shows the situation for the verbal–imagery style.

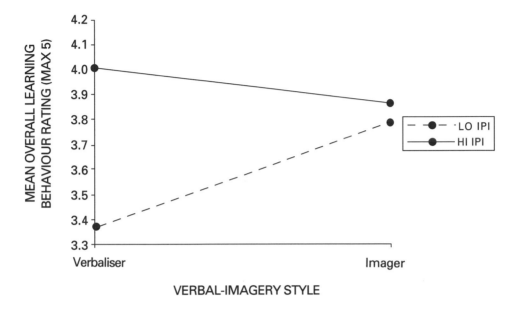

Figure 4.8 Learning behaviour memory and verbal–imagery style

Inspection of Figure 4.8 shows that with the verbal–imagery dimension of style, it is the verbalisers who are most affected by working memory capacity. Verbalisation is a more elaborated process than imaging and is likely to require more processing capacity. Again, superior performance is possible when there are adequate processing resources available for the verbalisers, while for the imagers, the performance is more average irrespective of the processing capacity.

Overall learning behaviour, memory and style

Working memory capacity has its major influence on the learning performance of analytics and of verbalisers. This is probably so because both of these style groups use a relatively elaborated method of processing information during understanding and learning. This elaborated approach produces good results and is effective, provided that there is sufficient processing capacity available to complete it. If capacity is inadequate then the processing is incomplete and learning performance is reduced.

By contrast, wholists and imagers probably employ a more economical method of processing, which may be more intuitive or impressionistic, that arrives at decisions without fully and exhaustively analysing all information, but by a processing sampling the incoming information. This approach produces reasonable performance, but at a level that is inferior to the approach used by analytics and verbalisers. However, since is it much less processing capacity intensive, it is much less affected by working memory capacity.

The method used by analytics and verbalisers is inadequate if there is insufficient capacity since information would be lost or the final conclusion not reached, resulting in poor performance. From a practical point of view, individuals with low memory capacity, and particularly those who are also analytics and verbalisers, can improve their performance by means of the load being reduced or the capacity enhanced by decreasing stress.

Riding, Dahraei, Grimley and Banner (2001) found that effective working memory capacity was critical with memory load sensitive subjects such as science, music, technology, art and geography, and particularly with analytics in subjects such as mathematics, English and history, and verbalisers in languages and religious education.

In summary, the wholist and the imagery operations are less demanding of memory than those of analytics and verbalisers. However, these former styles are generally associated with less good academic performance, and where there is adequate memory the analytic and verbalisers are superior.

Overall learning conclusions

The picture is still incomplete but may be summarised as follows.

The structure of the material to be learned interacts particularly with the wholist–analytic style dimension:

- Individuals of complementary style (wholist-verbalisers and analytic-imagers) are affected by the step size of the learning material and improve from large to small steps, while those of unitary style are not affected.
- Analytics need a large 'viewing window' compared to wholists, when dealing with information.
- There is an interaction between gender and wholist–analytic style in the facilitating effect of structure in the form of both headings and overviews, such that these most help male analytics and female wholists. By contrast,

male wholists and female analytics are more comfortable in situations that are closed and predictable and do not require divergent thinking.

With presentation mode, the verbal–imagery dimension is important:

- Imagers tend to learn better from pictorial presentations than verbalisers, while verbalisers learn better from verbal presentations than imagers.
- In terms of content type, individuals appear to learn best when the information can be readily translated into their preferred verbal–imagery mode of representation.
- Given a choice, imagers are attracted to material that contains illustrations while verbalisers prefer text. In doing work, the tendency by imagers to the use of pictures, and verbalisers writing, increases with ability.
- Basically with males, complementary groups were best on a separation of the channels of pictures and words received aurally, while the females were best on the single channel of picture and words. With the unitary groups, the males were best on a single channel, while the females were superior on separate channels.

Including working memory and style together shows that for overall learning:

- Working memory capacity has little effect for wholists but a large effect for analytics.
- Verbalisers are more affected by working memory capacity than imagers.

The implications of the findings for practical school learning will be considered in Chapter 7.

CHAPTER 5

Style and pupil behaviour

Chapter overview

This chapter will consider aspects related to cognitive style and behaviour.

Style and behaviour problems

- Wholists are likely to lack structure in their thinking, and thus have poor behavioural control. By contrast, analytics are structured and produce behaviours that are more controlled but that may exhibit frustration.
- Mainstream school behaviour studies have found that males have worse behaviour than the females, and that the male wholists have the worst behaviour.
- Studies of special schools show that male wholist and male verbaliser pupils predominate.

Style and types of problem behaviour

- In terms of sociability and problem behaviours, wholists who exhibit such behaviours will tend to be immature, disruptive and verbally aggressive, while analytics will be inclined to be loners, lack empathy, show physical aggression and have temper tantrums.

Pupil management

- Pupils need both care and appropriate control, for their own personal development.
- Wholists and analytics differ in the type of misbehaviour that they manifest, and they will benefit from different behaviour management strategies. Wholists need a stricter regime and analytics a more relaxed one.

Style and behaviour problems

As was noted in the introduction, several factors contribute to the standard of pupil conduct behaviour. These will include those associated with the home background and peer group values and pressures. This chapter will consider the individual characteristics of cognitive style in their effect on behaviour and the response of the school.

Style and social behaviour

Riding (1991) argued that for the wholist–analytic dimension, wholists are likely to be unstructured, global and inclusive in their thinking. This may manifest itself as lacking behavioural control. By contrast, analytics are structured but socially separate, resulting in behaviours that are generally more controlled but that may exhibit frustration and intensity, and they may be socially unaware and exclusive.

On the basis of a consideration of social behaviour, it might be expected that the conduct behaviour of wholists would be worse than that of analytics since the former are both less well organised with respect to both self-control and learning, and more outgoing than the latter. Several studies have indicated that this is so.

Style and mainstream school behaviour

Riding and Fairhurst (2001) asked teachers to rate the behaviour and home background of 9–11-year-old pupils from a primary school, in a fairly deprived urban area. Both ratings were on a five-point scale as follows: 1 Very Poor; 2 Poor; 3 Moderate; 4 Good; 5 Very Good. The results are shown in Figure 5.1.

Riding and Burton (1998) with 14–16-year-old pupils, asked the form/tutor-group teachers of the pupils in each school, who had generally known the pupils over several years, to rate the classroom behaviour of each child on a five-point scale from 1 to 5 where 1 was the worst behaviour and 5 the best. The pupils had been with the same form/tutor-group teachers over several years. The intention was to obtain an overall global impression of conduct behaviour. The teachers were likely to be influenced in their rating by outward active manifestations of misbehaviour such as verbal interruption, distracting other pupils, inappropriate moving about, or physical aggression to other pupils or the teacher. Passive misbehaviour, such as inattention, was not likely to be counted since it was not disruptive. There was a significant relationship

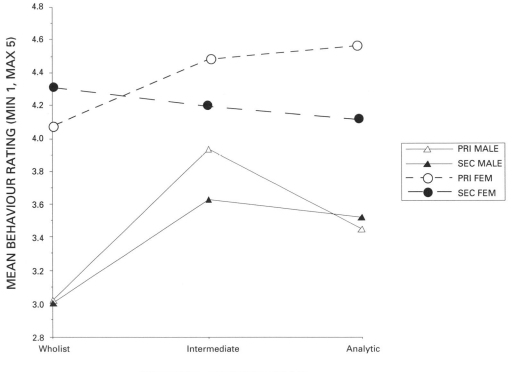

Figure 5.1 Behaviour ratings for age range, gender and wholist–analytic style groups

between wholist–analytic style and behaviour for the secondary school pupils as shown in Figure 5.1.[7]

Inspection of Figure 5.1 indicates that the males had worse behaviour than the females, and that of the males the wholists had the worst behaviour, and that this applied to both the primary and the secondary male pupils in a similar manner.

A study of 15–18-year-old pupils in ten Kuwaiti secondary schools (Riding and Al-Hajji 2001) indicated that when pupil self-perception was also assessed, the poorest conduct behaviour was by the low self-perception male wholists. This study, which also assessed the educational background of the parents, suggests that, as argued in the introduction, many variables interact in affecting behaviour. For instance, when self-perception is high, it is the male analytic-verbalisers who behave least well, although not as badly as the male low self-perception wholists.

---

[7] Adapted from Riding and Burton (1998), and Riding and Fairhurst (2001).

Style and special schools

Style and referral of pupils to special schools

Riding and Craig (1998) assessed the style of 83 boys aged 10–18 years in two residential special schools to which the pupils had been referred because of behaviour problems. They found that their style on the wholist–analytic dimension was skewed to the wholist end of the continuum relative to a comparison sample of 413 male pupils in ordinary secondary schools. In order to contrast the distribution for the special school pupils on each style dimension with that of the comparison group, the two dimensions were divided on the basis of the style ratios of the comparison group into three divisions with equal numbers of comparison group students (i.e. 33.3 per cent) in each.

There was a significant effect of wholist–analytic style and of verbal–imagery style, and there was no significant interaction between the style dimensions or with school. In other words the style effects apply to the pupils from both schools, and independently for each dimension. The percentages of special school pupils in the divisions on the style dimensions are shown in Figure 5.2.[8]

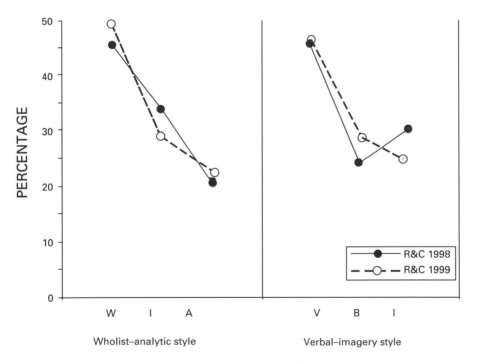

Figure 5.2 Style of special schools pupils in terms of comparison group

---

[8] Adapted from Riding and Craig (1998; 1999).

Inspection of Figure 5.2 indicates that the proportion of wholists and of verbalisers was greater in the special school sample than the comparison sample which had equal proportions in each division (i.e. 33.3 per cent).

In a further study of 131 male 11–16-year-olds in eight special schools, Riding and Craig (1999) found very similar results as shown in Figure 5.2.

Inspection of Figure 5.2 indicates that wholists and verbalisers predominate in special schools.

Style and truancy

Rayner and Riding (1996) studied 17 15–17-year-old pupils attending a truancy unit because of their previous failure to attend school. Again comparison with a control sample showed a significant difference on the wholist–analytic dimension, as shown in Figure 5.3.[9]

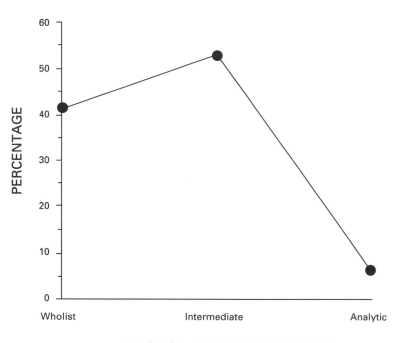

Figure 5.3 Distribution of style of refusers

---

[9] Adapted from Rayner and Riding (1996).

Inspection of Figure 5.3 shows that the greater number of children attending the truancy unit were either wholists or intermediates.

Wholist–analytic style and psychoticism

Riding and Wigley (1998) in a study of 17–18-year-old college of further education students found that wholists (mean 3.27, sd 2.18) were significantly more psychotic than the analytics (mean 3.03, sd 1.81), who in turn were more so than the intermediates (mean 2.57, sd 1.81), although since the maximum possible psychoticism score was 12, all scores were modest. Cook (1993: 87) observed that the psychoticism scale probably measures a tendency to social deviance.

Conclusion

Studies of children in primary and secondary schools show that cognitive style is related to their classroom behaviour, with male wholists being the worst behaved. Further studies with pupils referred to special schools (EBD) confirm this view. Finally, a study with further education students indicated a relationship between psychoticism and wholist style. The poor behaviour of the male wholists is likely to be most prominent when other adverse factors, such as poor home background, low self-esteem, poor quality of schooling, are also present. When conditions are generally more favourable then there will probably be little difference between the style groups in terms of behaviour.

Style and the types of problem behaviour

In order to investigate behaviours associated with particular styles, Riding and Craig (1998) with 83 10–18-year-olds in two residential special schools studied the personal files of the 14 most wholist (ratio range 0.44–0.63) and 14 most analytic (ratio range 1.32–2.01) subjects; plus the 14 most extreme verbalisers (ratio range 0.59–0.93), and 14 most extreme imagers (ratio range 1.22–3.30) in the sample described above. These files contained personal information, including the Statement of Special Educational Need and current school reports, supplying pertinent details of the pupil's domestic, health, social, academic and psychological status. The comments made about them were grouped into three categories: (a) those referring to sociability, (b) those dealing with problem behaviours, and (c) those describing ability. Where the percentage exhibiting a behaviour was less than 30 per cent at both ends of a dimension, the item will be omitted since it did not represent a major behaviour, nor could it show a difference between the styles. The main effects were observed for the wholist–analytic dimension and only these will be considered here.

Sociability

Comments describing social behaviour, including external versus internal focus of activity, were ordered from high to low difference between the wholists and analytics. The order of the behaviours and the percentage reported as having the observed behaviours is shown in Figure 5.4.

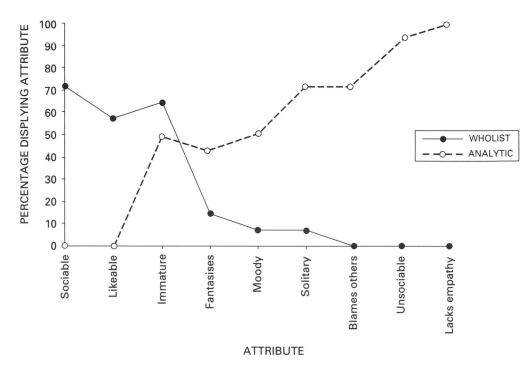

Figure 5.4 Behaviours associated with sociability

Inspection of Figure 5.4 indicates that wholists tend to be sociable and outward, while analytics are described as more unsociable and detached.

Problem behaviours

The reported problem behaviours were again arranged in a descending order of difference between wholists and analytics. The percentage reported as having the observed behaviours is shown in Figure 5.5.

Inspection of Figure 5.5 suggests that the wholists are inclined to be disruptive, often in a verbal manner, whereas the analytics display more anger and physical aggression.

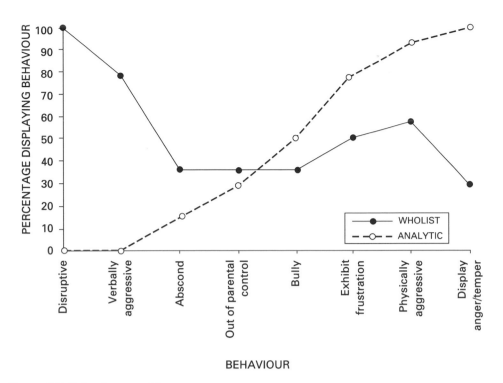

Figure 5.5 Behaviour problems

A further study was carried out by Riding and Craig (1999) with pupils aged 11–16 years from eight special schools. This considered all pupils and not just those at extremes of the style continua, and also included age as a variable. The disruptiveness of wholists increased with age but decreased for the analytics. Being a loner increased with age and analytic style. Verbalisers exhibited more temper tantrums than imagers. Home background also appeared as an important contributor with 87 per cent of the sample having at least one factor related to an adverse home environment. Adverse factors included, for example: no contact with either the father or the mother; evidence of sexual, physical or emotional abuse; neglect by the parents.

Conclusion

Where one or more other conditions, such as home background, peer values and school, are adverse then the pupils are likely to display problem behaviours. The form of manifestation of these behaviours will then depend on the style of the pupil – wholists and analytics are likely to display different types of problem behaviours. Wholists will tend to be immature, disruptive and verbally aggressive, while analytics will be inclined to be loners, lack empathy, show physical aggression and have temper tantrums.

If, on the other hand, other conditions are at a satisfactory level, then the effect of style will largely be on learning behaviour and learning performance as considered in Chapter 4.

The effect of wholist–analytic style on conduct behaviour will probably depend on the level of the conditions of the home, the peer culture and the quality of the school, as shown schematically in Figure 5.6.

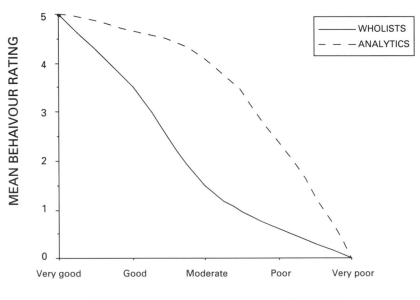

Figure 5.6 Probable behaviour for wholist–analytic style and quality of factors

When the quality is very good then there will be little difference in the behaviour of the wholists and the analytics. As quality falls, the wholists will be affected first since they lack an internal control and their behaviour will noticeably decline. As the quality becomes very poor, there will again be little difference except that the wholists and analytics will differ in the ways in which misbehaviour is manifested, with the wholists being more outwardly disruptive. A consequence of this is that wholists are more likely to be referred to special schools.

Pupil management

Effective learning is dependent on pupils both behaving reasonably and learning effectively. These two requirements are interdependent – poor behaviour reduces learning performance, while failure to learn has a detrimental effect on self-perception, reduces motivation and can therefore increase misbehaviour. Furthermore, significant conduct misbehaviour by just one or two pupils can have a very disruptive effect on the learning performance of the whole group.

Pupil needs

Pupils need both care and appropriate control with clear rules and expectations, in both their own personal development and efficient learning in the school. Table 5.1 shows the possible effects of two basic aspects of teaching on pupils of different styles.

Table 5.1 Pupil need and cognitive style

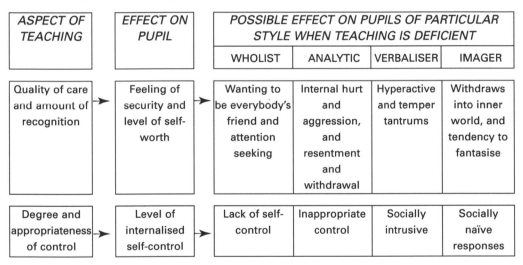

ASPECT OF TEACHING	EFFECT ON PUPIL	POSSIBLE EFFECT ON PUPILS OF PARTICULAR STYLE WHEN TEACHING IS DEFICIENT			
		WHOLIST	ANALYTIC	VERBALISER	IMAGER
Quality of care and amount of recognition	Feeling of security and level of self-worth	Wanting to be everybody's friend and attention seeking	Internal hurt and aggression, and resentment and withdrawal	Hyperactive and temper tantrums	Withdraws into inner world, and tendency to fantasise
Degree and appropriateness of control	Level of internalised self-control	Lack of self-control	Inappropriate control	Socially intrusive	Socially naïve responses

Teachers need to provide both care and control. The cognitive style of the teacher may affect:

- the type of relationship with pupils;
- the expectations about their behaviour.

All pupils will need outward encouragement. If the teacher is analytic-bimodal, analytic-imager, intermediate-bimodal or intermediate-imager then the natural relationships with pupils may be more distant, and these teachers may need to make a positive effort to be more outwardly encouraging, rather than assuming that pupils know that they feel their work is good.

With respect to expectations about behaviour, wholists and verbalisers are likely to be more informal while analytics and imagers are more formal in setting and expecting clear boundaries. Pupils, particularly if they are wholists, will benefit from clear behavioural boundaries as described in the next section.

The development of appropriate approaches

Approaches need to be developed that are appropriate to the different style groups.

Wholist–analytic dimension

It has been shown that wholists and analytics differ in the type of misbehaviour that they manifest, and they will benefit from different behaviour management strategies.

Wholists tend to lack a natural inclination to structure their thinking and so may be without an internalised control unless it is externally imposed. This is more likely when the home background is deficient. They will benefit from an approach that provides a clear structure for behaviour and a means of internalising it. Generally, wholists need clear rules and their strict enforcement so that they are more externally organised and restricted. Wholists will need to be encouraged to internalise structure.

Analytics are more likely to have an internal structure of rules and will be less troublesome whatever the regime. However, in some cases when the individual is under stress as when there are problems at home, the structure is likely to become more intense and may be inappropriate, in which case they may need a regime that corrects this with appropriate behaviours. Analytics need to find ways of releasing frustration by being more open, so that there is not a build-up that leads to an emotional outburst. Analytics need a freer regime and praise and recognition to help them to feel more externally open and free.

It may be that wholists need a stricter regime and analytics a more relaxed one.

Verbal–imagery dimension

Verbalisers are likely to be more outwardly active and prefer a more externally dynamic type of activity. By contrast, imagers will be more inward-looking and may have a less real view of the world, and will be happy with a quieter environment.

In terms of managing pupil behaviour the main concern will probably need to be with the wholist–analytic dimension.

Conclusion

Studies of pupils in mainstream schools indicate that cognitive style is related to their classroom behaviour, with male wholists being the least well behaved. Investigations of pupils referred to special schools (EBD) show that male wholists and verbalisers are in the majority. Further, a study with further education students indicated a relationship between psychoticism and wholist style.

The poor behaviour of the male wholists is likely to be most in evidence when other adverse factors, such as poor home background, low self-esteem, poor quality of schooling, are also present. In cases where conditions are more favourable then there will probably be little difference between the style groups in terms of behaviour.

Where one or more of the conditions, such as home background, peer values and school, are adverse then the pupils are likely to display problem behaviours. The form of manifestation of these behaviours will then depend on the style of the pupil – wholists will tend to be immature, disruptive and verbally aggressive, while analytics will be inclined to be loners, lack empathy, show physical aggression and have temper tantrums. If, on the other hand, other conditions are at a satisfactory level, then the effect of style will mainly be on learning behaviour and learning performance.

Teachers need to provide both a caring environment and one with clear boundaries. It may be that wholists with behaviour problems need a strict regime while analytics benefit from a more relaxed one.

CHAPTER 6

Long-term memory

Chapter overview

This chapter will consider the role of long-term memory in learning.

Building a structure of knowledge

- Long-term memory has a very large capacity and the information in it is organised into a structure. In meaningful learning the new matter is related to and fully incorporated into the organised structure of memory.
- The information in memory is organised and this ranges in complexity from the very simple linkage of two items to the highly organised structure of related concepts.

Integration of new information into the structure

- The purpose of learning activities is to ensure that learning is active and that the material is accommodated into memory. Learning activities can help the pupil to form links between the new material and what he or she already knows.
- Learning activities will be selected to facilitate active learning, to consolidate memory and subsequent recall, and to encourage strategy development.

Maintaining the availability of knowledge

- Periodic revision is required to maintain knowledge in memory.
- A *spiral curriculum* may be used in which, periodically, new information is learned and added to a series of basic concepts.

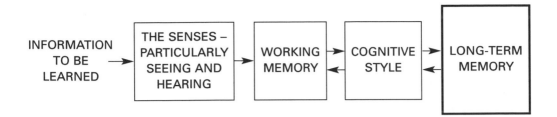

Building a structure of knowledge

Long-term memory is the repository of knowledge. In contrast to working memory, it has a very large capacity and the information in it is organised into a structure.

Meaningful learning

As noted in Chapter 2, Ausubel (1968) distinguished between meaningful and rote learning. In meaningful learning the new matter is fully incorporated into the organised structure of memory, while in rote learning the information is incompletely accommodated because the learner lacks the necessary related knowledge.

Ausubel has argued that meaningful learning is the most effective, in that it is easier to accomplish than rote, is better retained and, since it is properly organised in memory, can be more efficiently applied or transferred to new situations and problems.

Pupils give new information meaning in terms of what they already know. Consequently, what the pupils currently know that is relevant and related to the present lesson is the most crucial determiner of whether learning will be meaningful and hence successful. If a pupil is unable to relate the new information to what he or she already knows then it will be meaningless and either not learned or at best learned in a rote manner. This learning will not contribute to a structure of knowledge. It follows from this that a crucial principle for successful teaching is that the teacher should start each topic from where the pupils are at in knowledge terms.

Building a wall

There is some similarity between building a wall and building up a structure of knowledge in the learner's memory. In a wall each course of bricks can only be laid when the preceding course is in place. In building up a structure in memory each new subject matter 'brick' must only be presented to the learner when the 'bricks' onto which it is to be placed are in position.

A good wall

A poor wall

An unstable wall

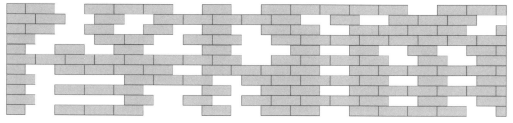

Figure 6.1 Building a structure

Figure 6.1 shows three walls. The first is a good wall with all the bricks in place. This would represent the ideal learning situation where all the related material is learned and built into a solid structure of knowledge.

The second wall is less satisfactory, several bricks are missing as would be the case where some aspects of a topic are not understood.

The final wall is very unstable and likely to collapse, and could not be a sound basis for further building upon it. Substantial parts are missing – as would be the case where a pupil had been badly taught or absent and had not learned the information to add it into the structure.

For the teacher it is vital to aim at meaningful learning, and in order to achieve this the pupils must have in memory the necessary relevant information before new learning begins.

The features of knowledge structure

A major purpose of education is to build within the pupil a structure of knowledge in long-term memory to enable critical thinking. The information in memory is organised. This organisation ranges in complexity from the very simple linkage of two items to the highly organised structure of related concepts. Three levels of structural organisation are:

- *Simple associations.* At the lowest level a link, or association, can be formed between just two items.
- *Concepts and attributes.* A concept like 'dog' will be linked to the attributes such as fur, tail, bark, paws and so on.
- *Conceptual structure.* Links can be made between a concept and those related to it. For example:

Labrador – dog – animal – living thing

All these types of structure occur in school learning. How they are formed and the organisations they produce will be considered.

Simple associations

The simplest learning is a link between two items. We have many such associations in memory. When you read, 'seven times seven', you automatically produce the response of '49', which you have linked to it. Similarly, the year 1066 evokes the name of a well-known battle, in a geographical context the name of a capital city like Paris brings the response of the country it is in, and in science, symbols such as H_2O give the substance they represent.

For an association to be learned the items must be presented together, or almost together, so that they are in working memory at the same time. They then enter long-term memory together and are stored as a linked pair. In ordinary learning situations, the strength of an association will depend on how frequently, and how recently, the items occur together. Hence, if multiplication tables or vocabulary lists are to be learned, they are presented with repetition and revision.

While it is possible for associations to be stored in memory in isolation from one another, in practice the aim in most school learning is to build up a structure of knowledge with the pupil's memory which will be conceptually organised.

Concepts and attributes

Too much information can be problematic. How does your processing system deal with Figure 6.2?

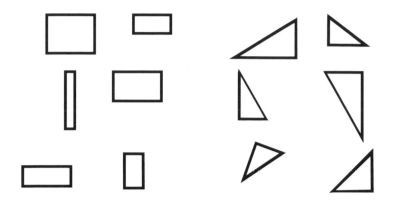

Figure 6.2 Twelve items of information

Although there are 12 quite different items, you try to reduce the information to be perceived by grouping the items according to similarities. You notice that half of the shapes have three sides, while the others have four. The next step is that you label them as triangles and rectangles respectively. This process of grouping is necessary if the memory is to cope with your environment.

The point has already been made in conjunction with working memory that our environment contains so much information, there is the danger that the information processing system will be swamped. In addition to limiting the entry of information, the problem is also overcome by reducing the amount of material that needs to be retained in memory, by grouping similar items under a common name or category to form a class concept.

You form concepts to reduce the amount of information your mind has to deal with, and this makes learning and thinking easier. A concept exists when you make the same response to a number of similar, but often different, stimuli. To all three-sided figures you make the same response of 'triangle'. Notice that the same response is made to similar, but not necessarily identical, stimuli.

Conceptual structure

Links are formed in long-term memory between concepts that are similar or related. These links may be because the concept can be included with other concepts under a common name, for example 'dog' and 'cat' subsumed under 'domestic animals', or it may be that a concept is dependent on others for its definition, for instance 'speed' is expressed in terms of 'distance' and 'time'.

Hierarchical organisation of class concepts

Concepts can be grouped in hierarchical form with the most inclusive at the top. Collins and Quillian (1969) suggested that the information in long-term memory is stored in conceptual groupings within a hierarchical structure, the position within the category being determined by the level of inclusiveness of the concept. Further, each item has those of its properties that are particular to itself stored with it and those that are general to the concepts in the same class or category are stored higher up the hierarchy with the superset (or more inclusive concept). An example given by Collins and Quillian was the concept of 'canary' (part of the hierarchy including 'canary' is given in Figure 6.3).

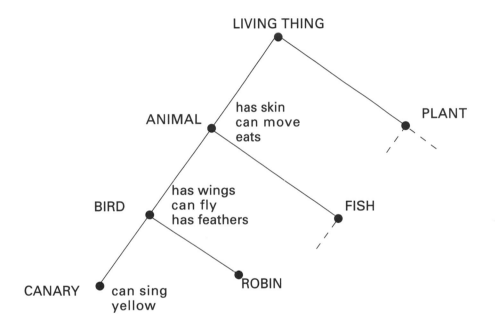

Figure 6.3 Hierarchical organisation of concepts (Adapted from Collins and Quillian 1969)

The attribute of 'flight' is stored with 'bird', the superset, since most birds can fly, whereas 'yellow' is stored with 'canary' since it is particular to that bird. They considered that incoming statements are checked by a search through the hierarchical memory structure until the necessary attributes are retrieved. They tested this by asking subjects to judge statements like 'a canary is a canary', 'a canary is a bird', 'a canary is an animal' (and many similar statements about other concepts) as true or false. Statements, both true and false, were presented in random order. The times a subject took to judge the statements were recorded and the means for the true statements were as follows. Statements about category membership took longer the further the concepts were apart in the hierarchy; statements like, 'a canary is a canary' took 1.00 second, a 'canary is a bird' 1.16 seconds, and 'a canary is an animal' 1.24 seconds. Similarly for the position of storage of attributes (i.e. 'a canary can sing', 1.31 seconds; 'a canary can fly', 1.39 seconds; 'a canary has skin', 1.47 seconds). It may be noted that attributes take longer to locate than category membership. These results may be interpreted as that class concepts are arranged in memory in a hierarchical fashion.

The structure of principles

A second way in which concepts are organised is in terms of their relationship to concepts that define them. Gagné (1970) has called such relational concepts 'principles'. Examples of principles are 'speed', 'volume' and 'density'. The organisation of principles is similar to that for class concepts, but instead of the concepts being included within class concepts within a category, a principle is based on other concepts that are related to it by a defining rule.

Consider, for example, the principle of 'speed'. Speed is the distance travelled divided by the time taken. Thus the idea of speed is built on the concepts of 'distance' and 'time' with the addition of the rule. Another instance is 'density'. The density of an object is its mass divided by its volume, and so density is dependent on 'mass' and 'volume' for its definition.

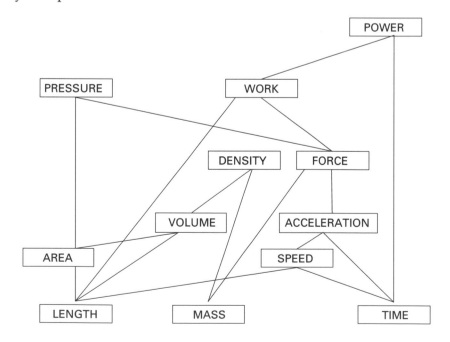

Figure 6.4 A structure of principles

An example of the way in which a structure of principles may be built up on a few basic concepts is given in Figure 6.4. Early in the primary school, children begin to become familiar with the fundamental ideas of length, time and mass. As they get older, onto these basic concepts they build the related principles of volume and acceleration and so on to the higher levels.

In reality, the memory structure of class and relational concepts is undoubtedly much more complex. The memory association networks are more elaborate with extensive connections. Further, memory involves the reconstruction of information in a dynamic way (see, for instance, Tulving and Craik 1999: Chapters 34–9). However, the simple illustrations serve to emphasise that there is an organised structure of knowledge, and this is the main educational implication of this type of research.

From a practical point of view the important thing to notice is that principles are dependent on other concepts for their meaning and cannot effectively be learned in isolation from one another.

Integration of new information into the structure

To facilitate the integration of new learning into what the pupil already knows, a series of learning activities may be used.

The purpose of learning activities

Learning activities have two purposes associated with building a structure of knowledge:

- to encourage active rather than passive learning so that the new material is integrated into what is already known;
- to aid memory of the material.

To some extent these purposes will overlap and an activity is likely to fulfil both of the above.

Effect of learning activity on recall

The activities pupils undertake during instruction may range from reading about the topic to expressing the information in their own words, or from looking at an illustration to making their own model or putting the material into dramatic form. In choosing activities the teacher should bear in mind the two basic reasons for employing them. The first is to ensure that learning is active and the second that the material is accommodated into memory.

There is the danger that material being learned may be only partially processed, with the consequence that it is not completely transferred to long-term memory and so not fully learned. Tasks done during learning will help the student to analyse information more fully. Further, information must not only be received into memory, but also related to relevant subsuming concepts, if the learning is to be meaningful, stable and is to form a structure of knowledge. The learning activity can help the student to form such links and to consider the relationships between the new material and what he or she already knows.

A basic principle that emerges from experimental studies of learning and retention is that while the input of information is essential to its reception, the output of the material is basic to its accommodation. Many teachers will have found that it is not until they come to explain a topic to their pupils that they realise the incompleteness of, and contradictions in, their own knowledge of it. Similarly, recalling and expressing information allows the student to consider the links between the material and related ideas. For this reason, more effective learning and retention results from the presentation of information followed by recall than from repeated presentation.

This principle has been demonstrated by several studies, although the learning material used was work lists rather than material more typical of school learning. Allen, Mahler and Estes (1969) visually presented university student subjects with a list of 27 noun–number pairs. When tested after 24 hours the percentage correct recall and the speed of recall was found to depend on the number of presentations as shown in Table 6.1.

Table 6.1 Percentage correct recall of number after word (adapted from Allen, Mahler and Estes 1969)

LEARNING ACTIVITY	PERCENTAGE RECALL ASSOCIATED NUMBER OF RETENTION INTERVAL (HOURS)		MEAN RESPONSE TIME IN SEC
	0	24	AFTER 24 HOURS
5 presentations	83	58	2.6
10 presentations	93	65	2.5
5 presentations plus 5 recall tests	91	82	2.1

It is seen that doubling the number of presentations did, as might be expected, improve learning, but from the teacher's point of view the interesting result is the effect of having five presentations followed by five recall attempts. During these five recalls no knowledge of results was given. There was very little difference in initial learning between the two methods, but the presentation plus recall resulted in much better over 24 hours and also quicker recall.

The results suggest that a learning activity that includes recall and output of the information being learned, produces a memory structure for the material that is both easier to retrieve and more stable.

Studies using prose material

Studies using prose material typical of school learning have compared repetition with no repetition, and immediate recall with no immediate recall, but not the relative effects on retention of additional presentation and recall.

In an early study, Peterson, Ellis, Toohill and Kloess (1935) gave groups of undergraduates a 25-line passage on the origins of monasticism in Western Europe. Control groups read the passage followed by immediate free recall. Other groups, after the initial reading and recall, received in addition either one or two further opportunities to read and recall immediately after the first reading and recall. The percentage recall by the groups at six and 18 weeks is given in Table 6.2. A different group was used for each treatment and retention interval.

Table 6.2 Recall of passage after different activities (Adapted from Peterson *et al.* 1935)

NO. OF PRESENTATION-RECALLS AT INITIAL LEARNING SESSION	PERCENTAGE OF DETAIL FREE RECALLED AFTER RETENTION INTERVAL (WEEKS)	
	6	18
1	32	29
2	40	35
3	55	44

It is seen that recall after both six and 18 weeks is directly proportional to the number of presentation-recalls because these activities resulted in better consolidated learning. In view of the findings of studies using word lists, it is likely that the recall part of the activity rather than additional presentations was responsible for the improved quality of the learning.

The consolidating effect of immediate recall alone was demonstrated by Spitzer (1939), who gave 11-year-old pupils eight minutes to study a 600-word passage about bamboo plants. One group were tested immediately and then after one week, while the other had no immediate recall. The percentage recall scores at the end of the week were, respectively, 48 and 32.

School learning activities

The basic principle, then, is that successful learning results from a combination of input and output. In school, activities that are frequently used include working out problems, expressing material in the pupil's own words, producing a picture or model to depict information and acting out events. All of these require the pupil to apply what he or she has in memory. Obviously the type of activity will depend on the subject matter and the age of the learner. Ten-year-olds doing a topic on the Tudor period might write about what they have heard, draw pictures depicting everyday life, make models of buildings and perhaps act out some notable historical event of the period. Secondary school pupils learning to solve equations in mathematics might be asked to explain the principle of finding the unknown term and required to work through a series of problems so that they can apply the methods.

It is important to note that, to be effective, the learning activity must involve the material in long-term memory. An activity such as copying a paragraph from a book, or to a lesser extent a picture, will probably not force the pupil to consider links between the new material and what he or she already knows.

The selection of learning activities

A range of activities will be used when teaching a topic that will cover all three purposes.

- *Active learning* – To facilitate active learning and integration of new material with what is known already, activities will include thinking about the new material and comparing it with what is already known, and looking for inconsistencies, by means of (a) working out problems, (b) expressing material in the pupil's own words (paraphrasing, summarising, etc.) and (c) applying the instruction to real situations.
- *Memory consolidation* – To consolidate and aid memory and subsequent recall, the following can be used: (a) inserted questions (self-test, quizzes, etc.) and (b) acting out events.
- *Strategy development* – Where appropriate it is advantageous to encourage strategy development to enable pupils to cope with situations that do not match their style. This in turn empowers pupils to cope with a wider range of materials.

Maintaining the availability of knowledge

Since new information is given meaning in terms of what the pupil already knows, it is important that the existing knowledge is both maintained and readily available for recall to relate to the new information.

Since information is forgotten over time, the teacher is faced with the practical problem of how to maintain material in the pupil's memory during the period between its first being learned, and such time as it should be recalled for relation with new learning or for a terminal test. Retention is maintained by means of revision and addition.

Revision

Let us suppose that the material a teacher presents will be recalled for, say, an examination in ten weeks' time. What form should the revision take and at what points during the retention interval should it be given? There are two forms of revision, retest and review, and these have different functions.

- *Retest* is requiring the pupils to recall the subject matter in order to maintain its availability in memory.
- *Review* involves re-presenting the subject matter, or a condensed version of it, in order to replace in memory any details that have been forgotten.

Obviously a retest will only maintain in memory what is still there and is of little use when much forgetting has taken place, but there is evidence that it is better than review at maintaining material in memory. The choice of revision method will therefore depend on how much forgetting has taken place.

Consider Figure 6.5, which shows a schematic retention graph. Information is forgotten more quickly to begin with and more slowly later on. Suppose the teacher has a revision session after two weeks by giving a retest of what was learned, this will maintain the availability of the material in memory and improve performance in the examination and will put back into memory much that has been forgotten.

Sones and Stroud (1940) looked at the relative effects of testing and review at various temporal positions during retention. Groups of 12-year-old pupils were given 20 minutes to read a 1,750-word article on the history of paper and methods of paper making. The groups were then given revision by either testing or rereading at a point during the seven-week retention period, after which a 40-item multiple choice test was given. The groups received the revision on either first and third days, eighth and fifteenth days, or fifteenth and seventeenth days. The revision test was a 30-item multiple choice test. The mean recall scores (out of 40) on the final test are given in Table 6.3.

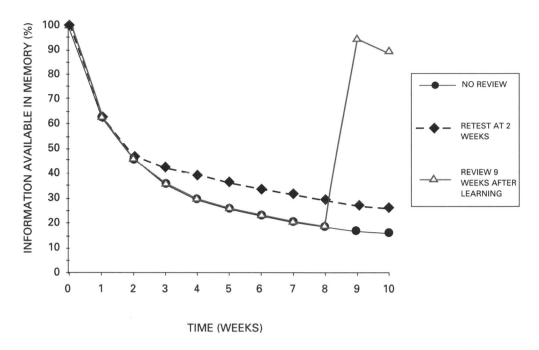

Figure 6.5 Schematic retention curves

Table 6.3 Mean score on test after seven weeks

TYPE OF REVISION	POSITION OF REVIEW AFTER LEARNING (DAYS)		
	1 and 3	8 and 15	15 and 17
Test	17.8	15.7	15.2
Rereading	16.0	16.4	16.9

It is clear that in their experiment the most effective revision was the test at first and third days. However, as has been suggested, testing became progressively less useful as the time since learning increased. By contrast, the effectiveness of rereading increased with time. While the exact placement of revision will depend on the particular material and the length of the retention interval, this experiment does guide the teacher in choosing and placing an appropriate revision activity.

Addition

As part of the normal learning process, material that was learned on a previous occasion is reconsidered and to it is added further new information. In other words, learning is cumulative. An infants school child learns about addition and then later, into this knowledge, incorporates the idea of multiplication. An older child may do a topic on Tudor England and then later some work on the Jacobean period, and this must be related to, and will involve, the recall of some of the previously learned material. At the secondary level a pupil learning about the physical concept of pressure will have to recall the concepts of force and area upon which the definition of this one depends.

Since new meaningful learning of necessity requires the recall of related information, a form of revision happens incidentally whenever further material is learned. The positioning of further learning, relative to the previous learning on which it depends, should be such that forgetting will not be too great otherwise formal revision will need to be incorporated.

Learning similar material

Not only will the temporal position of the new information be important, but also the way in which the new material relates to the existing will affect the retention of what had been learned previously. When the form and content of the new material is very similar to the existing material, the recall of the first learned material may be lessened. Kalbaugh and Walls (1973) gave groups of 13-year-old children several 210-word science passages about minerals which were very similar in content and format. Each dealt with a different mineral, e.g. quartz, calcite. Recall of the first passage immediately and after two days was compared with the number of passages interpolated between it and final recall. The recall performance on the randomly ordered item completion test is given in Table 6.4.

It is clear that learning similar, related material has a retroactive effect, and can make the recall of the initial learning difficult. It must be noted that this degree of similarity probably only occurs in the lists of properties of materials, and even there a teacher can do much to structure the material so that repetitive similarity is avoided.

Table 6.4 Recall of the first passage presented (Adapted from Kalbaugh and Walls 1973)

No. of interpolated passages	0	2	4
Recall after 2 days as percentage of immediate	91	78	72

Another aspect of the learning of similar materials was studied by Kalbaugh and Walls which compensates for the loss of the initial passage. They found that when similar passages are learned prior to the test passage, the greater the number of passages, the better the immediate recall of the test passage. This was attributed to a learning to learn effect.

Learning related material

When interpolated material is related, but dissimilar in structure, the effect on recall tends to be helpful. Ausubel, Stager and Gaite (1968) found that when learning is followed by interpolated material that is related in substance, so that cumulative learning typical of school can take place, then recall of the first passage is facilitated rather than hindered. In order to simulate a real learning situation, they had three learning materials, each approximately 2,000 words long – one on Zen Buddhism, another on Buddhism and a third on drug addiction. The first and second passages obviously contained related information, while the third did not. One group of student subjects read the Zen Buddhism passage for 40 minutes and then two days later the Buddhism piece, followed after three more days by a recall test of the first passage about Zen Buddhism. A control group followed the same pattern except that they received the drug addiction material in place of the Buddhism passage. Although the Buddhism passage did not provide any answers for the recall test, the experimental group had a higher recall score than the control (respectively 11.4 and 9.9 out of a maximum of 31).

It would appear that in usual school learning, the reception of information related to previous learning improves the availability of the subject matter in memory. This will be due in part to the revision effect, and also perhaps to an improvement in the organisation of the material in memory as it is built up into a more complete structure.

Spiral curriculum

The order in which information is presented will be influenced by the need for periodic review of what has already been learned. Information is forgotten with time, but with revision it can be maintained in memory. The precise intervals between review sessions will depend on the subject matter. In any case, in practice, most learning is cumulative. A typical learning sequence may be represented as follows: learn material A – recall A and learn related topic B – recall AB and learn related topic C – recall ABC and learn D, and so on.

With this sort of sequence in mind, Bruner (1960: 52) suggested a *spiral curriculum* in which, periodically, new information is learned and added to a series of basic concepts.

A schematic view of a spiral curriculum is shown in Figure 6.6. A topic begins at the centre of the spiral with the presentation of the three main related topics A, B, C and D with instruction at a high level of generality (Level 1) to give an overall view of the topic. Progressively, through Levels 2 and 3, the areas are presented at a more specific level in a cyclic manner so that each area is revised and extended.

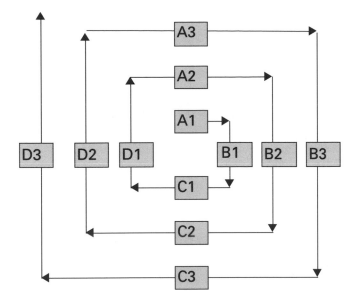

Figure 6.6 A spiral curriculum

Pupils are likely to benefit from a spiral curriculum presentation in which concepts are repeatedly presented starting at a fairly general inclusive level and progressively becoming more specific.

Conclusion

In summary, long-term memory is where the knowledge is stored in a structured and related form. New learning is given meaning in terms of what is already known and new information is integrated into this structure. However, information is liable to loss through forgetting and needs periodic maintenance by revision.

CHAPTER 7

Learning design and behaviour management

Chapter overview

This chapter will consider aspects of style related to the design of learning and the management of behaviour.

Style of teaching delivery

- Effective teaching involves the use of teaching styles that will appeal to a range of pupil cognitive style.
- How effectively a person learns will depend on the extent to which the instructional material, and the way it is presented, matches their cognitive style.

Planning a topic and its delivery

- What pupils see and hear is understood in terms of what they already know.
- Effective learning means allowing pupils enough time to process the new information.
- Pupils learn best when the structure of the material suits their cognitive style.
- Learning is easier when the presentation suits their cognitive style.
- Learning is more complete when pupils actively engage with the new material.

Managing behaviour

- There is the need to develop methods of managing pupil behaviour in the classroom.
- Pupils require a combination of meaningful learning, recognition and control.

Style of teaching delivery

Having set out the evidence for the basic principles of learning and teaching in the preceding chapters, these will now be applied to the practical teaching situation. Whatever your current experience of teaching, there is always some room for improvement. It is also useful to reflect on how you teach, because in doing so you may come upon some simple way of making your teaching more effective and also more efficient. Further, consideration of your own teaching style and the cognitive style and working memory performance of your pupils may indicate possible reasons why some of them succeed while others do less well.

This chapter will consider the components of teaching style and how you might modify your 'natural' teaching style by developing other teaching strategies. Your teaching style will largely consist of your style of teaching delivery and pupil management. The aim is to provide a style-friendly approach to learning! It is not only what you teach that is important, but how you teach it.

In planning teaching in the past, you will have been influenced by your own cognitive style, since you will have assumed that the ways in which material is structured that you find easy to learn will also have applied to your pupils. Similarly, you will have tended to think that the mode of presentation that you find best will have been shared by your pupils. Furthermore, you will have been inclined to consider that learning activities that you have found useful will be those that appeal to and help your students.

At one level these were reasonable assumptions since you had only your own introspective experience to go on, although you may have been frustrated on occasions to find that however many times you explained things to some pupils, in a manner that seemed exceedingly plain and obvious to you, they still did not appear to understand. The descriptions about cognitive styles and the way they work should have shed some light on this experience.

Consider two pupils, Jane and Jill.

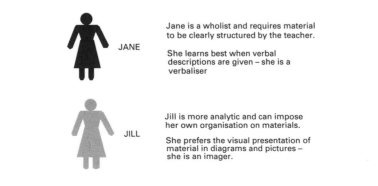

JANE — Jane is a wholist and requires material to be clearly structured by the teacher.

She learns best when verbal descriptions are given – she is a verbaliser

JILL — Jill is more analytic and can impose her own organisation on materials.

She prefers the visual presentation of material in diagrams and pictures – she is an imager.

How will these two pupils approach learning? How will your teaching style relate to their cognitive styles?

As has been pointed out, an individual's cognitive style affects the manner in which information is habitually processed during learning and thinking. Consequently cognitive style affects the ways in which an individual finds it easiest to learn. Pupils taught with materials and methods that do not match their cognitive style will therefore find difficulty in learning.

Your pupils will have a range of styles and only a few of them will have the same style as yourself. Consequently your 'natural' teaching style will often not match the cognitive style of the majority of your pupils, and this is likely to make their learning less efficient.

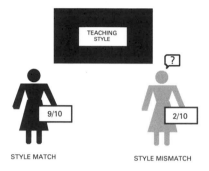

Effective teaching involves the use of teaching styles that will appeal to a range of pupil cognitive style. How effectively a person learns will depend on the extent to which the instructional material, and the way it is presented, matches their cognitive style. There is the need to develop your teaching style to suit a broad range of pupil cognitive style.

In order to consider styles of teaching it will be useful to remind ourselves of the basic steps necessary for effective learning within the context of individual differences in style. If pupils have problems it could be argued that much of the problem is with the delivery and not with the pupil.

Considering individual pupils and their learning

Are some pupils finding your subject or topic difficult? Obviously there can be several reasons why a pupil is not succeeding with a subject. The causes, acting singly or together, can include:

- They have not learned essential aspects of the subject in the past through absence or poor teaching.
- They have limited working memory capacity.

- Their cognitive style is not ideally suited to the subject matter.
- They are finding it difficult to concentrate on their work because of emotional problems caused by, for example, trouble at home.

Knowledge of the styles of the pupils permits a consideration of whether their difficulty with your subject is because of their style. You might find it helpful to select the four pupils in your class who do worst and/or have an unsatisfactory level of conduct behaviour, and consider their style. For these pupils note their styles and plan some future curriculum activities which may help them to learn more easily and suit the needs of their style in terms of improving behaviour.

You could be helped in your considerations by using the *Cognitive Styles Analysis* (Riding 1991) and *Information Processing Index* (Riding 2000a) to assess your own performance and that of your pupils.

Planning a topic and its delivery

As a way of moving forward this section will provide guidance for activities aimed at producing a wider range of teaching strategies suitable for all the style groups. The planning of a topic will comprise the following stages.

1. *Starting point.* The topic should be ordered starting from what is known by the pupils, and in such a way that the ideas are introduced progressively like building a wall. The selection of the material to be taught and its starting point needs to fit in with what the pupils already know, to enable meaningful learning.
2. *Pace.* Adjust the rate of the presentation to allow slower pupils to keep up and to accommodate the new learning. Be aware of the limitations for information processing of the pupil's working memory.
3. *Structure.* The choice of the way in which it will be structured to facilitate understanding. The structure should suit the cognitive style of the pupil. For wholists, it should enable the parts to be identified, and for the analytics, a whole view should be obtained.
4. *Presentation mode.* The selection of the mode of presentation of the material to maximise ease of learning. Some adaptation of the content may be necessary to help pupils whose style means that they find it difficult to represent the material in its present form. Both verbal and pictorial presentation should be used so that both the verbalisers and the imagers are catered for.
5. *Learning activities.* Various types of learning activities to be used to consolidate the learning, and to develop learning strategies. Hence, learning activities should be chosen to:

- integrate learning into existing knowledge,
- consolidate it in memory, and
- help the development of learning strategies which allow styles to cope with difficult situations.

6. *Behaviour management.* In so far as it is possible and appropriate, care and recognition and a clear behavioural structure should be provided, particularly for pupils where the home background does not supply these.

These will be considered in turn.

(1) Curriculum sequence

PRINCIPLE 1: What pupils see and hear is understood in terms of what they already know.

What makes learning meaningful?

With pupils of all styles, for new learning to be understood it must be linked to what pupils already know. Difficulties in learning occur if pupils are presented with information that they cannot relate to existing concepts in their memory. If they learn it at all, they will learn by rote and the new material will be stored as an isolated unit, which is difficult to make use of in a range of contexts.

The pupil's present knowledge and effective learning

Successful learning, like constructing a wall, needs something on which to build. What has already been built is what the pupil currently knows that is relevant to the new topic, and that will give meaning to the new information. As with building a wall, each new topic may only be added if the ones on which it depends for meaning are already in place. As the wall progresses, each block must be capable of being built upon those already in place. Any missing bricks are those not learned or forgotten. Poor instruction is like a poor wall, where many of the blocks are missing – the pupil has only understood and learned some of the information.

The first step in planning instruction is to compare the content of what is to be taught, with what the pupil already knows that is relevant to the topic. This will give their knowledge readiness characteristics. This present knowledge will indicate the starting point for the new learning. The teacher must be aware of what the pupils already know about the topic that is necessary to the understanding of the new work. For instance, they cannot be taught how to solve simultaneous equations until they can cope with ordinary equations.

While this sounds very obvious it is often undertaken too infrequently and superficially by many teachers. For new learning to be efficient an essential condition must be fulfilled. The pupil must already have acquired the necessary concepts to which the new material can be related. The new information will need to be accommodated and integrated into what the pupil already knows so that the relationship with other ideas and contexts are established. This will be done by means of the learning activities.

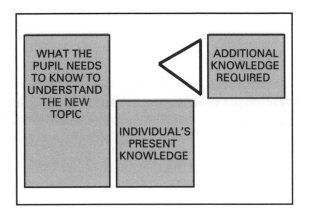

Figure 7.1 Starting point for new learning

Knowledge readiness of the pupils
Take these steps to check that your pupils are ready for the new topic, and that the 'supporting blocks' are in place.

What is the conceptual content of the new topic?
Before commencing a new theme or topic, identify the concepts that are necessary to make the topic meaningful to your pupils. List the main ideas/information that the new topic assumes will be known.

What is the existing pupil knowledge?
Consider the group of pupils who are going to receive the new topic. To what extent are they familiar with these ideas? If they have not been covered previously, adjust your starting point to include the missing ideas. These will need to be learned before embarking on the main theme, so that the new information can be efficiently received.

How readily available is that knowledge?
It is also important to bear in mind that even if information has been covered previously, this does not necessarily mean that it will be remembered. In view of this, consider the present knowledge that the pupils have relevant to the

new topic. It needs to be capable of being readily recalled. It is sensible to make the new topic overlap with the previous one to which it is related, in order to remind your pupils of the necessary concepts.

Is any revision necessary?
If there is a difference between what the new material requires to give it meaning, and what the pupil presently knows, then this difference must be made up before teaching the new topic.

(2) The limitations of working memory

> **PRINCIPLE 2: Effective learning means allowing pupils enough time to process the new information.**

As already noted, while information is being received and analysed in working memory it is very vulnerable to loss by displacement by the input of further information. Limited working memory capacity particularly affects analytics and verbalisers. As a pupil listens to the teacher, for instance, while he or she is analysing the sentence just heard there is the danger that it may be displaced by the next sentence he or she hears. Further, the individual will not be conscious of this loss, except that the loss will not make sense. Teachers may improve learning efficiency by the following: (a) reducing the information processing load, (b) increasing the available capacity of working memory, (c) adapting the presentation structure and mode to suit the pupil's cognitive style.

(a) Information processing load reduction
Some cognitive style groups are more memory critical than others because they use a fairly elaborated method of processing information. This particularly applies to memory load sensitive subjects such as science, music, technology, art and geography, and to analytics in subjects such as mathematics, English and history, and verbalisers in languages and religious education.

The processing load can be reduced by several methods.

(i) Use of external representation
External representation is where notes or jottings are used as an external memory into which information is concisely placed for ready retrieval at a glance, thus reducing the load on working memory, during activities such as learning and problem solving. Encourage the use of external representation during learning in the form of notes and diagrams.

(ii) Reducing processing load
Slowing presentation. Slowing the rate of presentation of information will help all pupils, and particularly those style-critical groups. At a simple level this can be done by reducing the rate of presentation of speech to allow more time for processing. Slowing can be either by speaking more slowly or putting pauses after sentences or paragraphs. This improves listening comprehension.

Using revision. Information processing efficiency can be improved by revising key concepts at the start of a lesson or a topic. Frequent revision may be employed so that the necessary concepts for giving meaning to the new work are readily available in long-term memory and primed for retrieval. This makes retrieval quicker and reduces processing load.

Sequence design. The subject matter being presented can be made more logical for the individual and hence easier to process. A comparison may be made between learning a list of items in the correct order with learning a list that has to be re-ordered at the same time while learning

(b) Capacity increased by reducing stress
The effective capacity of working memory is also affected by the level of anxiety a pupil is experiencing. Anxiety reduces working memory performance, probably because some of the capacity is devoted to the objects of anxiety, and this reduces the resources available for general processing. Anxiety in a pupil may result from a number of factors – unhappiness at home because of a domestic upset, problems with peers, pressure from teachers.

If stress increases anxiety, which in turn reduces the working memory capacity, then there is the problem that this reduction causes misunderstanding, confusion and uncertainty when processing information. This, in turn, causes additional stress and hence further increases anxiety. There will thus be a degree of cyclic effect.

Some pupils are more vulnerable to stress than others, and for pupils who are naturally anxious, reassurance from teachers can sometimes be helpful. Stress reduction may follow from the use of approval and recognition, and reducing unnecessary pressure to achieve, particularly in nervous pupils. Again this particularly applies to memory load sensitive subjects such as science, music, art and geography, and to analytics in subjects such as mathematics, English and history and verbalisers in religious education and language.

(c) Presentation structure and mode
The teacher should be aware that some cognitive style groups are much more working memory critical than others because they use a fairly elaborated method of processing information. Limited working memory capacity particularly affects analytics and verbalisers.

Since there is less effect of memory capacity on the performance of wholists and of imagers in several subjects, these can be helped in other ways – wholists by modifying the structure of the material to be learned by the use of overviews and organisers, and imagers by the adjustment of the mode of presentation from verbal to pictorial.

(3) Structure and wholist–analytic style

PRINCIPLE 3: Pupils learn best when the structure of the material suits their cognitive style.

The structure of the topic

We have already noted that wholists can see the whole but have more difficulty seeing the parts, and that analytics are good at seeing the parts but have problems with integrating it into the whole. We need to be aware of the difference between pupils of different styles.

Remember that the way you naturally tend to structure material will reflect your own style. You will need to make a conscious effort to have a broader approach.

Is the purpose of the topic clear to you? Make sure that you have a clear view of where the topic is leading and why it is being taught. If your intention is uncertain to you, then it is not likely to be clear to your pupils!

Have you a clear view of the structure of the topic? Consider the structure of the topic, and identify its principal parts and how these fit together. Produce an analysis of the topic by listing the headings and sub-headings on an A4 sheet. Use this as the basis for an *organiser* to show the overall structure of the parts and the sections. This will be particularly useful to give wholists an indication of the parts of the topic.

Can an overview be used to make the purpose clear to the pupils? The topic you will teach will probably be presented over a period of several weeks. If possible, at the end, give an indication of the scope of the topic to help, particularly analytics, to see a whole view of the subject matter and how the parts fit together. It may help pupils to be provided with a single sheet *overview* of the topic at this point.

In practice, the easiest method of having a teaching style that appeals to a range of styles is to provide both an *overview* and an *organiser*.

Organisers and overviews

It is necessary to incorporate into the teaching, opportunities for emphasising both the whole and the parts. Just how this will be done will depend upon the

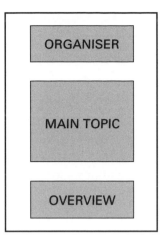

Figure 7.2 Organisers and overviews

subject, but in general an *organiser* can be used to show the structure of the parts, and an *overview* to give the whole view.

Wholists will need help in seeing the structure and sections of learning material, and of dividing the whole into its parts. They will need an *organiser* to show them the parts of the whole and to enable them to analyse the material into sections. They will be inclined to see the overall view when it is recalled from memory, but will be able to distinguish the parts when the material is set out before them, with the sections very clearly marked. The approach would be to use an organiser of the content of all topics emphasising the sections, or parts, and their divisions (e.g. hierarchical content map showing subdivisions).

By contrast, analytics are helped by an *overview* to provide them with the whole structure, to enable them to integrate the parts into a whole. It is probable that they will need to have all the material, facts or information laid out before them in order to get a picture of the whole, so that it does not depend on memory. When recalling information, because their memory will tend to focus on only one part at a time, they may not be able to get a whole view. They will require an overview of the whole content of all the topics emphasising the structure and links, to enable them to appreciate it as a unified whole (e.g. integrated concept map showing links).

Implications for teaching. Adjusting structure to style is most easily done for the wholists by having an *organiser* to indicate the parts and structure of each topic into which the whole can be analysed. For the analytics an *overview* is used to provide a picture of the whole topic into which the parts are linked. Both the *organiser* and *overview* can be delivered before and again after the topic.

Table 7.1 Wholist–analytic style and support required

STYLE	ORDER OF PRESENTATION	TYPE OF SUPPORT REQUIRED
Wholist	Parts to whole to parts	An organiser to indicate the parts and structure of the material, into which the whole can be analysed.
Analytic	Whole to parts to whole	An overview to provide a picture of the whole of the material into which the parts can be linked. Analytics need a structure/map into which to fit new information to show its interrelationship.

Although it is an over-simplification, telling the pupils about what they are to hear roughly corresponds to giving an *organiser*. Telling them what they have been told will be similar to an *overview*. Basically:

- first you tell them what you are going to tell them;
- then you tell them;
- then you tell them what you have told them.

Layout of information and wholist–analytic style

With respect to the way in which information is presented, analytics will find tables and tree diagrams helpful in structuring the information, but wholists will not. Since wholists find the extraction of information from densely embedded displays difficult, these should be avoided as the only means of conveying the information.

(4) Mode of presentation and verbal–imagery style

PRINCIPLE 4: Pupils learn best when the presentation suits their cognitive style.

In terms of the choice of mode of presentation of material, generally imagers learn better from pictorial presentation and verbalisers from written material. When pupils receive information whose presentation does not match their cognitive style then performance in learning is likely to be impaired, particularly when the material is more difficult for the pupil or more complex in nature.

Verbal–imagery style and the type of content

With respect to type of content, generally verbalisers are likely to be superior on the understanding and recall of information that contains unfamiliar and acoustically difficult terminology. This is a situation frequently met when a new technical subject is first encountered. They are also better on details dealing with actions, time and abstractions. The style of the verbaliser would appear to be more appropriate to coping successfully with learning from text and definitions, than that of the imager.

Imagers do best on the material that can be visualised in mental pictures, and that does not contain many acoustically complex and unfamiliar terms. They are superior to verbalisers on spatial and directional information.

The basic principle that applies is that information is likely to be successfully understood and learned if pupils can readily code it using their natural styles. Further, when the content of the material does not coincide with the cognitive style, then learning performance will be reduced, particularly if the pupil is unable to find ways of representing the information in a form that corresponds to their style.

The mode of presentation should be as appropriate as possible to the styles of the pupils. Many types of information can be presented in several ways. A wide variety of media is available for instruction, and consideration should be given to how this can be most effectively used to provide a wide range of modes to suit a variety of styles. Printed material can contain both text and illustrations. Live presentation by a teacher can use both speech and pictures or objects. Video or multimedia technology will provide both modes.

Social preferences

Verbalisers will benefit from a more stimulating presentation than imagers. They will prefer variety and will be more reluctant than imagers to plod through material they find boring. They are also more happy to learn in a social group, while imagers are often happy to work alone.

If you are a verbaliser then you are likely to use speech and textual material more than pictorial material. You may need to make more effort to accommodate the needs of the imagers in your classes. If you are an imager, your presentations are likely to emphasise the visual and you may neglect textual versions of your material. However, your teaching is likely to be interactive and you prefer, and are sensitive to, feedback from your pupils.

Choice of mode of presentation

Is the topic likely to be difficult for some styles to represent in their natural style mode? Examine the content of the topic to see whether there are parts of it that, in their present form, are only in one mode. Consider how other forms of

Table 7.2 Verbal-imagery style and support required

STYLE	TYPE OF SUPPORT REQUIRED	ACTION
Verbaliser	Provide verbal versions of pictorial and diagrammatic material. Verbal in terms of text and speech. Lively and outgoing in manner of delivery.	Tell me.
Imager	Convert verbal material into pictorial form. Choose concrete analogies of abstract ideas. Use of pictures, illustrations, diagrams, charts and graphs. Less bothered about a dynamic presentation.	Show me pictures.

representing the information may be possible. For instance, in mathematics, a problem could be expressed in verbal form as:

An athletics track has two straights, each 90m long, and two semicircles, each 110m long. Calculate the total length of the track.

However, this same problem could also be presented symbolically or in pictorial form. Look for parallels within your subject that may help some pupils.

What modes of presentation are you going to use? If you are a verbaliser, then your natural inclination will be to use speech and textual material to the exclusion of pictorial material. You need to make more effort to accommodate the needs of the imagers in your classes. If you are an imager, your presentations are likely to emphasise the visual and you may neglect textual versions of your material.

What are the possible presentation modes that could be used? It is important to note that many types of information can be presented in several ways. A wide range of media are available for instruction, and consideration should be given to how these can be most effectively used to provide a wide range of modes to suit a variety of styles.

- Printed material can contain both text and illustrations.
- Overhead transparencies and slides can contain both words and diagrams.
- Live presentation by a teacher can use both speech and pictures or objects.
- Video and multimedia technology will provide both modes.

Try to present material in both verbal and pictorial forms where possible; aim at dual mode presentation!

(5) Learning activities

PRINCIPLE 5: Pupils learn best when they actively engage with the new material.

Learning activities have three purposes:

- to encourage active rather than passive learning so that the new material is integrated into what is already known;
- to aid the memory of the material;
- to facilitate strategy development so that pupils will find ways of coping with material that is not ideally suited to their styles.

Active versus passive learning

As has been noted, for learning to be meaningful, it must be actively learned and linked to what the pupil already knows. This is in contrast to passive, rote learning, where the pupil may internalise information without linking it into the structure of what he or she already knows. For learning to be complete, new information must not only be transferred to long-term memory but also be linked to the relevant related material already there. If it is accepted into the memory without being properly integrated into the structure, the new learning will be rote. The information will be stored in isolation from other items and hence will be difficult to retrieve.

Pupils can sit and listen to a teacher, but this does not mean that they are actually learning. Learning activities should be chosen to ensure active learning and integration of the new information and skills into what is already known. Every effort should be made to ensure that the pupils have the opportunity to accommodate new learning as fully as possible into what they already know. Wholists may be inclined to undertake passive learning more easily and may require activities that encourage active integration of the new material into what they already know. This can be done through the use of the appropriate learning activities.

Remembering

The basic principle is that successful learning results from a combination of the input of information, and the output of responses to it. Activities should require people to apply or express what they have in their memories. It is important to note that, to be effective, the learning activity must involve interaction with the material already in long-term memory. An activity should encourage the pupils to consider the links between the new material and what they already know. This is likely to improve subsequent recall.

Choice of learning activities

What are the reasons for using learning activities? Learning activities have at least three purposes:

- to encourage active rather than passive learning so that the new material is integrated into what is already known;
- to aid memory of the material;
- to encourage strategy development so that a pupil will find ways of coping with material that is not ideally suited to their style.

To some extent these purposes will overlap and an activity is likely to fulfil more than one of the above.

How should learning activities be selected? Select a range of activities for your topic that will cover all three purposes, bearing in mind the requirements of pupils of different styles.

Table 7.3 Learning activities

Purpose	Learning activity	Examples of specific activities
Active learning: To facilitate active learning and integration of new material with what is known already.	Thinking about the new material and comparing it with what is already known, and looking for inconsistencies.	(a) working out problems (b) expressing material in the pupil's own words (paraphrasing, summarising, etc.) (c) applying the instruction to real situations
Memory consolidation: To consolidate and aid memory and subsequent recall.	Tests and questions.	(a) inserted questions (self-test, quizzes, etc.) (b) acting out events
Strategy development: To encourage the development of strategies to enable the pupil's style to cope with a range of material even when it is not ideally suited.	(a) Translation into other representations. (b) Mismatch – dealing with material in the 'wrong' form for the learner's style.	(a) writing a brief overview to obtain a whole view (b) constructing a one-page organiser of a section of a topic to see the parts (c) representing material in their preferred mode (e.g. an imager producing a picture from a verbal description)

Where appropriate it is advantageous to encourage strategy development to enable pupils to cope with situations that do not match their style. This in turn empowers pupils to cope with a wider range of materials.

Developing teaching strategies

We have noted that, if the instructional material is meaningful to the pupil and easy to learn because its structure and presentation is adjusted to match the pupil's style, then there is likely to be success at learning and nothing succeeds like success! A happy pupil is a successful pupil! Success enhances self-confidence and makes further learning attractive.

Matching presentation style to the cognitive style of the pupil is particularly important for pupils of lower ability, or when the task is complicated and the material is relatively difficult for the pupil. This is because, in these cases, there is more pressure on the pupil's learning system, and consequently danger of overloading them with information to be learned. This raises the question of when the teacher should focus on matching and when on strategy development, for a particular group of pupils, as shown below.

Table 7.4 Matching and strategy development

Ability	Approach
Low	Match presentation to style
Moderate and high	Develop strategies for situations not ideal to style

Managing behaviour

As was noted in Chapter 5, studies of pupils in schools suggest that cognitive style is related to their classroom behaviour, with male wholists and verbalisers being the least well behaved.

Where one or more of the conditions, such as home background, peer values and school, are adverse then the pupils are likely to display problem behaviours. The form of manifestation of these behaviours will then depend on the style of the pupil – wholists will tend to be immature, disruptive and verbally aggressive, while analytics will be inclined to be loners, lack empathy, show physical aggression and have temper tantrums. If, on the other hand, other conditions are at a satisfactory level, then the effect of style will mainly be on learning behaviour and learning performance.

Teachers need to provide both a caring environment and one with clear boundaries. Wholists with behaviour problems probably need a strict regime, while analytics benefit from a more relaxed one.

Behaviour Control Strategies

There is the need to develop methods of managing pupil behaviour in the classroom, which includes the necessary aspects of teaching – care, recognition and control.

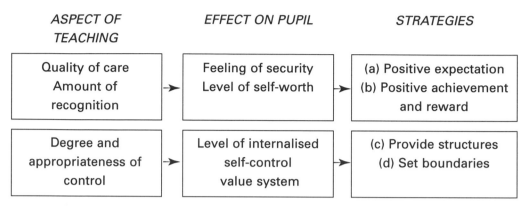

Figure 7.3 Care, recognition and control

The emphasis would be on both care and acceptance of pupils on the one hand, and control and structure on the other, since a balanced development requires the inclusion of both. A very caring approach may lead to indulgence, while a heavily controlling regime results in oppression; neither facilitates self-discipline.

Intervention for pupils showing behaviour problems and finding difficulty with the subject will need to combine actions to improve understanding with those aimed at care and control, and could include the following, each of which will have both a teacher and a pupil focus.

Establish a positive expectation and direction for individual differences in learning.

- *Teacher:* Raise the awareness of pupils for the implications of their styles for learning. Negotiate individually designed style-led attainable targets/tasks for specific pupils to aim at in their school work.
- *Pupil:* Recognise their style-based learning preferences, strengths and limitations.

Identify the strategies by which the targets may be achieved and recognised.

- *Teacher:* For individual students, according to their style, specify learning activities, their structure, the order in which they are to be done, and modes of presentation, in order to attain agreed goals.
- *Pupil:* Be clear about the tasks to be done, and the strategies that are to be employed to maximise the efficiency of style.

Provide behavioural structures, by emphasising order, routines and patterns.

- *Teacher:* Establish a set of behaviours in specific contexts, such as coming to order at a particular point, doing work in a particular way, being neat, tidying away at the end of each activity.
- *Pupil:* Following set instructions and routines; completing tasks and activities aimed at reinforcing the learning of patterns of behaviour.

Set behavioural boundaries, by having clear rules, constraints, restraints, stressing social conventions and expected behaviour.

- *Teacher:* Make overt the rights, rules, responsibilities and routines to be observed in the classroom.
- *Pupil:* Activities aimed at developing and understanding the rights, rules and responsibilities in school.

Conclusion

Effective teaching involves the use of teaching styles that will appeal to a range of pupil cognitive style. Pupils understand new learning in terms of what they already know. Effective learning means allowing pupils enough time to process the new information. Pupils learn best when the structure of the material suits their wholist–analytic style. Learning is easier when the presentation suits their verbal–imagery style. Learning is more complete when pupils actively engage with the new material. There is the need to develop methods of managing pupil behaviour in the classroom, particularly when other conditions such as the home and the peer group are less favourable. Pupils require a combination of meaningful learning, recognition and control.

CHAPTER 8

Developing pupil learning strategies

Chapter overview

This chapter will consider the development of pupil learning strategies.

The distinction between style and strategy

- Cognitive styles are in-built, habitual in use and fairly fixed. By contrast, learning strategies may be developed by the pupil to help in situations where their style does not naturally fit the task being done.
- The need to use strategies increases as ability is less and/or the task processing load or complexity increases.

The formation of learning strategies

The development of strategies consists of the following three:

- Sensing and preferring – to an extent students will be aware of the degree to which they are understanding the learning they are receiving.
- Selecting – pupils need to be encouraged to use whatever learning means seem to be right for them as individuals.
- Learning strategy formation – three types of strategy contribute to learning: translation strategies, adaptation strategies and strategies that aim at a reduction of the processing load.

Facilitating the development of learning strategies

- Pupils should be encouraged to consider what modes and structures they prefer.
- They can be shown examples of learning strategies using translation, adaptation and load reduction.

- Pupils need to feel confident to use whatever means seem to be right for them as individuals.
- They can be given tasks that do not match their style with the encouragement that they should try to find ways of translating the mode or the material to suit their style.

There is the need to encourage pupils to become *independent learners*. An important aspect of this is that they have the ability to choose and use the way they learn best. Thus they need to be helped to develop a range of learning strategies and to have the freedom that the 'right way' to learn is the one that suits them best.

This chapter will consider how pupils can develop learning strategies, as a step towards becoming independent learners, to help them in situations where their natural style is inappropriate. In doing this it is necessary to:

- distinguish between style and strategy;
- know how learning strategies are formed;
- consider how individuals can be helped to develop strategies to apply to learning situations.

The distinction between style and strategy

Learning strategies

Cognitive styles are in-built, habitual in use and fairly fixed. By contrast, *learning strategies* may be developed by the pupil to help in situations where their style does not naturally fit the task being done.

In learning situations where the style matches the task then the individual will find learning relatively easy. However, where the task differs in type from their style then the individual will find learning more difficult. For instance, when a task requires an overall broad view, an analytic will have difficulty in seeing the big picture. When the material is highly verbal then the imagers may find it harder.

Since cognitive styles appear to be fairly fixed, individuals are either blessed or lumbered with them depending on the type of tasks they are undertaking. They cannot change their styles but they can develop strategies to make them as effective as possible for a particular learning situation. Pupils need to be encouraged to develop learning strategies which enable them to use their styles as effectively as possible in a range of situations, and particularly when the situation does not naturally lend itself to easy use by the style.

The following are examples of strategies that may be used to help individuals accommodate situations and learning to their style.

- An imager may 'translate' a page of text into a diagram which represents the same information in visual form.
- A verbaliser may describe a picture with words.
- An analytic wanting a 'whole' view of a topic may map out the elements on a large sheet of paper.
- A wholist may go through a chapter of a book and list the headings to give an indication of its structure.

When strategies are important

Both style and intelligence are thought to be relatively fixed for an individual. However, an individual can develop learning strategies to mitigate any limiting effects of both style and intelligence and these improve learning performance. There is evidence that more intelligent students are better at developing strategies then less intelligent ones, and will do so without external intervention. Yet lower ability pupils are most likely to need to use strategies in order to achieve at least modest academic performance. The need to use strategies increases as ability is less and/or the task processing load or complexity increases, as shown in Figure 8.1.

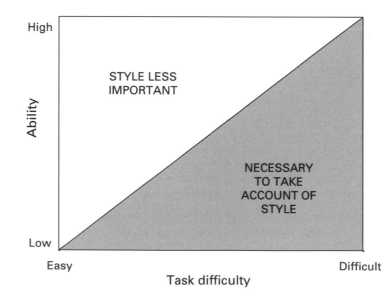

Figure 8.1 Ability, task complexity and style

In order to improve the learning performance, particularly of less intelligent students, there is the need to find ways of helping them to develop appropriate learning strategies in order to improve their learning performance and hence their educational attainment.

The formation of learning strategies

The development of learning strategies will involve the interaction of relatively fixed individual characteristics with the learning activity. Riding and Sadler-Smith (1997: 11) argued that individuals may not be able to change their styles but they can develop strategies to make themselves as effective as possible in a given learning situation.

The development of strategies consists of the following three stages:

1. sensing and preferring,
2. selecting,
3. learning strategy formation.

(1) Sensing and preferring

When faced with a learning situation, individuals will sense inwardly the extent to which they feel comfortable with the situation. They may not be very aware of this in a conscious sense of saying to themselves that they feel unhappy, but with respect to certain aspects of learning they will have a sense of the extent to which the learning task is easy or more difficult. This awareness by the student will be with respect to at least three aspects of the learning situation:

- the mode of presentation of the learning task;
- the structuring of the task;
- the social context of the learning.

Ease of use of the mode of presentation

Riding and Staley (1998) gave a questionnaire to university business studies students which assessed their preferences about the content and presentation of their courses, and this was compared with the actual performance by students on the course modules. Basically, where the mode of presentation and course content matched the verbal–imagery style of the student, then the students underestimated their performance. In cases where the verbal–imagery style did not match, they overestimated their performance.

This was interpreted as suggesting that while the performance of students is affected by the extent to which the mode of presentation matches their verbal–imagery style, they are not very consciously aware of the match or mismatch, during actual learning.

However, where students are given an actual choice of mode of presentation, they will choose the one that suits their style. Riding and Watts (1997) told secondary school students that three versions of a sheet giving information on study skills had been prepared for them, and that each sheet contained the same information but that the formats were different. They were then invited to come one at a time to take one of the versions which were laid out on a table. The versions were unstructured-verbal (paragraphs, without headings), structured-verbal (paragraphs, each with a clear heading) and structured-pictorial (paragraphs, each with a clear heading, and a pictorial icon depicting the activity placed in the left margin). No students chose the unstructured-verbal version. With the two structured versions, the majority of the verbalisers selected the verbal version and most of the imagers chose the pictorial. Students were obviously attracted to, and preferred to select, materials that appeared to them to suit their own style.

It appears, then, that students are likely to sense which format of learning material or presentation they prefer, even if they do not actually feel less comfortable when learning from some inappropriate presentations.

Appropriateness of the structure

In the study by Riding and Staley, described above, where there was a match between the structural requirements of the subject matter and the wholist–analytic style of the students, then the students did less well than they expected, but better than they expected when there was a mismatch. This was interpreted as indicating that the students were sensitive to how easy it was to understand a subject and were consciously aware of the style of structure preferred, and expectation was commensurately higher or lower.

Students will be aware of the extent to which they are understanding the teaching they are receiving.

Suitability of the social situation

Riding and Read (1996) individually questioned secondary school pupils about their preferences about learning and working in social contexts. The preferences for group and individual working were that work in groups was particularly liked by wholists, while individual work was least disliked by analytics. Sadler-Smith and Riding (1999) in a study of the effect of cognitive style on the learning preferences of undergraduates found further support for this.

The first step to strategy attainment is the awareness that particular formats or situations are more helpful to, and more comfortable for, the individual. Pupils should be encouraged to consider what modes and structures they prefer. This then forms the basis for the next stage.

(2) Selecting

As individuals become increasingly aware of what suits them in learning, if they have the opportunity they begin to select the most appropriate mode or structure, where possible or when a choice is provided. For example, an imager may prefer to focus on a picture in a book rather than on the text. Riding and Read (1996) asked secondary school pupils about their preferences as to mode of working. Imagers reported that they used less writing and more pictures than verbalisers, especially where the subject allowed, as in science. The tendency by imagers to use pictures, and verbalisers writing, increased with ability. There was evidence that lower ability pupils were more constrained by the usual format of the subject than were those of higher ability.

This development of a strategy of selecting the mode or structure which, for the individual, suits their style can then lead to more effective and conscious strategy development. An important feature here is that there is no 'right' way to learn that applies equally to all individuals. Teachers need, therefore, to avoid the notion of 'this is the way' to learn. After all, a particular teacher's natural teaching style will be a reflection of their own cognitive style.

Pupils need to be encouraged to use whatever means seem to be right for them as individuals. This can be quite a liberating experience for pupils!

(3) Learning strategy formation

There are at least three key types of strategy which contribute to the enhancement of learning by utilising an awareness of style. These strategies use different functions:

- translation strategies;
- adaptation strategies;
- strategies that aim at a reduction of the processing load.

Translation
Translation involves recasting the information, which as presented may be in a form that does not suit an individual's style, into a mode that makes it easier

to process and understand. Examples of such translations include the following.

By changing the mode of presentation to match the position on the verbal–imagery dimension. For instance, a verbaliser could change pictorial information into words, and the imagers could change words to illustrations or diagrams.

- A verbaliser may describe a picture or diagram with words.
- An imager may 'translate' a page of text or a verbal description into a diagram which represents the same information in visual form. The mathematical concept of an equation can be represented visually by a picture of a balance with the equals sign at the fulcrum or pivot, and this may aid imagers.

By using external representation. Wholists can be encouraged to divide general concepts into specific points. Analytics may be helped by setting information out on a sheet in parts and re-ordering it into a whole structure. If a person is an analytic then they will have difficulty in seeing the whole of some task or situation. They can be encouraged to develop the strategy of mapping it out on a sheet of paper so that they can lay out the whole, which will allow them to see all parts at once rather than concentrating on the separate aspects.

- A wholist may go through a chapter of a book and list the headings to give an indication of its structure.
- An analytic may set out the elements of a topic on a sheet of paper to provide a 'whole' view.

All of these are attempts to represent the information in a form that is more appropriate to the style of the learner.

Adaptation

This is where a style dimension is pressed into service because a function is not available on the other dimension of an individual's style.

The verbal–imagery representational style can often be pressed into service to help with an individual's limitation in the wholist–analytic dimension. For instance, an analytic-imager obviously does not have the same facility as a wholist to obtain an overview of situations or information. However, an analytic who is also an imager may use the overall view that a mental image allows to provide a more whole view of a topic by generating an image of the whole.

Similarly, a wholist-verbaliser lacks an analysing facility, but the analytic nature of verbal representation may to some extent be used as a substitute. Thus, a wholist who is also a verbaliser may use the aspect of verbalisation that divides concepts into discrete units, as an analyser to help to determine the parts of the material.

Some possible adaptations are shown in Table 8.1.

Table 8.1 Available styles for the four groups[10]

Type	Cognitive style	Styles available by adaptation
Complementary	Wholist verbalisers	Wholist and analytic
	Analytic imagers	Analytic and wholist
Unitary	Analytic verbalisers	Analytic only
	Wholist imagers	Wholist only

It will be observed that only those of complementary style have the possibility of adaptation while those of unitary style do not.

Reduction of processing load

Here the approach is to minimise the information processing load by using a strategy that economises on processing. As noted in Chapter 2 on working memory, although we are not usually consciously aware of it, any information we see or hear we have to analyse and process in order to give it meaning. This analysis takes processing capacity within working memory. If the information is in the preferred mode then the information processing load is less than if it is not. For an individual, additional processing load will, at the least, result in a longer time being required to learn the information. At worst, the load may exceed capacity, and the information may not be learned at all.

Some examples of strategies to reduce the load are as follows:

- An imager who finds that verbal processing imposes a high load can selectively scan text and extract only the most important sections to save reading the whole.
- A wholist could underline words in text to produce 'headings' to clarify the structure.

The development of individualised learning using multimedia computer presentation offers the possibility of the student controlling the rate of presentation of information.

Facilitating the development of learning strategies

A specific programme of strategy development aimed at the teaching of learning strategies could form part of the personal and social education of pupils. The approach used will depend on the ability and age of the pupils.

---

[10] Adapted from Riding and Sadler-Smith (1997).

(1) Preference awareness

Pupils should be encouraged to consider what modes and structures they prefer. An important first step – sensing – towards a strategy is for individuals to be aware of their own style and of its strengths and limitations, and then to recognise that the tasks they find difficult are often so because of a mismatch between the task demands and their style. This is important in freeing them from the sense of inadequacy that often accompanies finding something difficult or failing at it. If a person acknowledges that they are likely to find certain types of task difficult and that they will never be brilliant at them because of their style combination then they will cease to feel so inadequate.

For pupils who are aged 14 years and above, cognitive style awareness is useful. The *Cognitive Styles Analysis* (Riding 1991) can be used to make pupils aware of their style, together with suggestions of its strengths and limitations, together with possible strategies to be used. Pupil feedback sheets could be developed from those given in the Appendix of the *Making Learning Effective* package (Riding 2000b).

(2) Selection

Pupils need to be given freedom to select and use whatever means seems to be right for them as individuals. This will require the teacher to actively recognise that there is not a single right way to learn, and to give pupils latitude to make their own choices of the best methods for them. The next step is then to encourage individuals to develop learning strategies to make tasks easier by using the strengths and features of their styles to help them.

(3) Strategy instruction

Pupils can be shown examples of learning strategies using translation, adaptation and load reduction, as described above. The intention will be the development of a repertoire of learning strategies.

(4) Use of style mismatch tasks

Pupils can be given tasks that do not match their style with the encouragement that they should try to find ways of translating the mode or the material to suit their style. For instance, verbalisers can be given pictures and imagers can be provided with text, with the instructions that they should try to put the information into a form that they find easiest to learn.

Over time and with experience and encouragement an individual will develop a range of strategies which contribute to their repertoire. This repertoire will comprise a combination of the variety of learning strategies employed by the individual. These strategies once devised can be stored and reused.

Resources

To enable teachers to develop teaching strategies a range of resources are available. These include the following which are available from Learning and Training Technology (UK Phone: 0121-429 7026).

Assessment instruments

Cognitive Styles Analysis (Riding 1991). The CSA is designed to assess the two fundamental dimensions of cognitive style.

Information Processing Index (Riding 2000a). The IPI is a self-scoring computer-presented assessment of working memory performance.

Both assessments are computer-presented, very simple to understand, applicable to a wide age (minimum age approximately 10 years) and ability range. They are suitable for a variety of cultural and situational contexts. They are both self-scoring.

Professional development

Making Learning Effective Package (Riding 2000b). This is a combined CSA and IPI package which is designed to facilitate professional development in teachers by raising their awareness of their own teaching style, and of the range of cognitive styles and information processing performance of their students.

The modules are supplied on the disk in Microsoft Word for Windows format. They are copyright but may be printed as required by the Licensee for use with the application.

The *Making Learning Effective Package* comprises: a one-year site licence for the school for both the CSA and the IPI, and the following modules:

- *Staff Development Manual (Cognitive Style and Effective Learning)*;
- *Development Co-ordinators Manual* containing instructions for the implementation of the programme.

References

Allen, G. A., Mahler, W. A. and Estes, W. K. (1969) 'Effects of recall tests on long-term retention of paired associates', *Journal of Verbal Learning and Verbal Behavior* **8**, 463–70.

Ausubel, D. P. (1968) *Educational Psychology: A Cognitive View*. New York: Holt, Rinehart and Winston.

Ausubel, D. P., Stager, M. and Gaite, A. J. H. (1968) 'Retroactive facilitation in meaningful verbal learning', *Journal of Educational Psychology* **59**, 250–5.

Baddeley, A. D. (1986) *Working Memory*. Oxford: Oxford University Press.

Baddeley, A. D. (1990a) *Human Memory: Theory and Practice.* Hove: Lawrence Erlbaum Associates.

Baddeley, A. D. (1990b) 'The development of the concept of working memory: Implications and contributions of neuro psychology', in G. Vallar and T. Shallice, *Neuro Psychological Impairments of Short-term Memory*. Cambridge: Cambridge University Press.

Baddeley, A. D. (1999) *Essentials of Human Memory*. Hove: Psychology Press.

Baddeley, A. D. (2000) 'Short-term and working memory', in E. Tulving and F. I. M. Craik (eds) *The Oxford Handbook of Memory*. New York: Oxford University Press, 75–92.

Baddeley, A. D., Gathercole, S. and Papagno, C. (1998) 'The phonological loop as a language learning device', *Psychological Review* **105**, 158–73.

Baddeley, A. D. and Hitch, G. (1974) 'Working memory', in Bower Gordon (ed.) *Human Memory, Basic Processes*. New York: Academic Press.

Baddeley, A. D. and Logie, R. H. (1992) 'Working memory: The multiple-component model', in P. Shah and A. Iiyake (eds) *Models of Working Memory: Mechanisms of Active Maintenance and Executive Control*. Cambridge: Cambridge University Press.

Bowlby, J. (1988) *A Secure Base*. London: Routledge.

Brown, B. B., Eicher, S. A. and Petrie, S. (1986) 'The importance of peer group ("crowd") affiliation in adolescence', *Journal of Adolescence* **9**, 73–96.

Bruner, J. S. (1960) *The Process of Education*. Cambridge, Mass.: Harvard University Press.

Calvo, M. G. and Eysenck, M. W. (1996) 'Phonological working memory and reading in test anxiety', *Memory* **4**, 289–305.

Cantor, J. and Engle, R. W. (1993) 'Working memory capacity as a long-term memory activation: An individual differences approach', *Journal of Experimental Psychology: Learning, Memory, and Cognition* **19**, 1101–14.

Carroll, J. B. (1993) *Human Cognitive Abilities: A Survey of Factor-Analytic Studies.* Cambridge: Cambridge University Press.

Charlton, T. and George, J. (1993) 'The development of behaviour problems', in T. Charlton and K. David (eds) *Managing Misbehaviour in Schools.* London: Routledge.

Collins, A. M. and Quillian, M. R. (1969) 'Retrieval time from semantic memory', *Journal of Verbal Learning and Verbal Behavior* **8**, 240–7.

Collins, N. L. and Read, S. J. (1990) 'Adult attachment, working models and relationship quality in dating couples', *Journal of Personality and Social Psychology* **58**, 644–63.

Conway, A. R. A. and Engle, R. W. (1994) 'Working memory and retrieval: A resource-dependent inhibition model', *Journal of Experimental Psychology: General* **123**, 354–73.

Cook, M. (1993) *Levels of Personality.* London: Cassell.

Cooper, P., Upton, G. and Smith, C. (1991) 'Ethnic minority and gender distribution among staff and pupils with emotional and behavioural difficulties in England and Wales', *British Journal of Sociology of Education* **12**, 77–94.

Daneman, M. and Carpenter, P. A. (1980) 'Individual differences in working memory and reading', *Journal of Verbal Learning and Verbal Behavior* **19**, 450–66.

Daneman, M. and Carpenter, P. A. (1983) 'Individual differences in integrating information between and within sentences', *Journal of Experimental Psychology: Learning, Memory, and Cognition* **9**, 561–84.

Daneman, M. and Tardif, T. (1987) 'Working memory and recall skill re-examined', in Coltheart, M. (ed.) *The Psychology of Reading.* Hove: Lawrence Erlbaum Associates.

DES and Welsh Office (1989) *Discipline in Schools: Report of the Committee of Enquiry Chaired by Lord Elton.* London: HMSO.

Douglas, G. and Riding, R. J. (1993) 'The effect of pupil cognitive style and position of prose passage title on recall', *Educational Psychology* **13**, 385–93.

Douglas, G. and Riding, R. J. (1994) 'Cognitive style and gender differences in drawing from memory versus copying in 11-year-old children', *Educational Psychology* **14**, 493–6.

Downey, D. (1995) 'Understanding academic achievement among children in stephouseholds: the role of parental resources, sex of stepparent, and sex of child', *Social Forces* **73**, 875–94.

Durbin, D., Darling, N., Steinberg L. and Brown, B. B. (1993) 'Parenting style and peer group membership among European-American adolescents', *Journal of Research on Adolescence* **3**, 87–100.

Elliman, N. A., Green, M. W., Rogers, P. J. and Finch, G. M. (1997) 'Processing efficiency theory and the working memory system: Impairments associated with sub-clinical anxiety', *Personality and Individual Differences* **23**, 31–5.

Engle, R. W., Cantor, J. and Carullo, J. J. (1992) 'Individual differences in working memory and comprehension: A test of four hypotheses', *Journal of Experimental Psychology: Learning, Memory, and Cognition* **18**, 976–92.

Eysenck, M. W. (1992) *Anxiety: The Cognitive Perspective.* Hove: Lawrence Erlbaum Associates.

Eysenck, H. J. and Eysenck, S. B. G. (1991) *Eysenck Personality Scales.* London: Hodder and Stoughton.

Gagné, R. M. (1970) *The Conditions of Learning*, 2nd ed. New York: Holt, Rinehart and Winston.

Gardner, H. (1983) *Frames of Mind: The Theory of Multiple Intelligences.* New York: Basic Books.

Gathercole, S. E. and Baddeley, A. D. (1993) *Working Memory and Language.* Hove: Lawrence Erlbaum.

Griffin, E. and Morrison, F. (1997) 'The unique contribution of home literacy environment to differences in early literacy skills', *Early Child Development and Care* **127**, 233–43.

Hopko, D. R., Ashcraft, M. H. and Gute, J. (1998) 'Mathematics anxiety and working memory: Support for the existence of a deficient inhibition mechanism', *Journal of Anxiety Disorders* **12**, 343–55.

Hulme, C. and Mackenzie, S. (1992) *Working Memory and Severe Learning Difficulties.* Hove: Lawrence Erlbaum.

Just, M. A. and Carpenter, P. A. (1992) 'A capacity theory of comprehension: Individual differences in working memory', *Psychological Review* **99**, 122–49.

Kalbaugh, G. L. and Walls, R. T. (1973) 'Retroactive and proactive interference in prose learning of biographical and science materials', *Journal of Educational Psychology* **65**, 244–51.

Levy, M. B. and Davis, K. E. (1988) 'Love styles and attachment styles compared: Their relationships to each other and to various relationship characteristics', *Journal of Social and Personal Relationships* **5**, 439–71.

Loeber, R. and Stouthamer-Loeber, M. (1986) 'Family factors as correlates and predictors of juvenile conduct problems and delinquency', in M. Tonry and N. Morris (eds), *Crime and Justice* (Vol 7). Chicago: University of Chicago Press.

Logie, R. H. (1995) *Visuo-Spatial Working Memory.* Hove: Lawrence Erlbaum Associates.

Luster, T. and McAdoo, H. (1996) 'Family and children influences on educational attainment: A secondary analysis of the high-scope pre-school data', *Developmental Psychology* **32**, 26–39.

McCord, J. (1979) 'Some child-rearing antecedents of criminal behaviour in adult men', *Journal of Personality and Social Psychology* **37**, 1477–86.

McKenna, F. P. (1984) 'Measures of field-dependence: Cognitive style or cognitive ability?' *Journal of Sociology and Social Psychology* **47**, 593–603.

Mruk, C. (1999) *Self-Esteem: Research, Theory and Practice*. London: Free Association Books.

Ogilvy, C. M. (1994) 'An evaluative review of approaches to behaviour problems in the secondary school', *Educational Psychology* **14**, 195–206.

Peterson, H. A., Ellis, M., Toohill, N. and Kloess, P. (1935) 'Some measurements of the effects of reviews', *Journal of Educational Psychology* **26**, 65–72.

Pistole, M. C. (1989) 'Attachment in adult romantic relationships: Style of conflict resolution and relationship', *Journal of Social and Personal Relationships* **6**, 505–10.

Pong, S. (1998) 'The school compositional effect of single parenthood on 10th-grade achievement', *Sociology of Education* **71**, 23–42.

QCA (2000) *Emotional and Behavioural Development Scale*. London: QCA.

Rayner, S. and Riding, R. J. (1996) 'Cognitive style and school refusal', *Educational Psychology* **16**, 445–51.

Riding, R. J. (1991) *Cognitive Styles Analysis*. Birmingham: Learning and Training Technology.

Riding, R. J. (2000a) *Information Processing Index*. Birmingham: Learning and Training Technology.

Riding, R. J. (2000b) CSA – Making Learning Effective. Birmingham: Learning and Training Technology.

Riding, R. J. and Agrell, C. (1997) 'The effect of cognitive style and cognitive skills on school subject performance', *Educational Studies* **23**, 311–23.

Riding, R. J. and Al-Hajji, J. (2001) 'The effect of home background, gender, cognitive style, and self-perception on school performance', in R. J. Riding and S. G. Rayner (eds) *International Perspectives on Individual Differences, Volume 2 – Self-Perception*, 267–82. Westport, Conn.: Ablex Publishing.

Riding, R. J. and Al-Sanabani, S. (1998) 'The effect of cognitive style, age, gender and structure on recall of prose passages', *International Journal of Educational Research* **29**, 173–85.

Riding, R. J. and Anstey, L. (1982) 'Verbal–imagery learning style and reading attainment in eight-year-old children', *Journal of Research in Reading* **5**, 57–66.

Riding R. J. and Ashmore, J. (1980) 'Verbaliser–imager learning style and children's recall of information presented in pictorial versus written form', *Educational Psychology* **6**, 141–5.

Riding, R. J. and Burton, D. (1998) 'Cognitive style, gender and conduct behaviour in secondary school pupils', *Research in Education* **59**, 38–49.

Riding, R., Burton, D., Rees, G. and Sharratt, M. (1995) 'Cognitive style and personality in 12-year-old children', *British Journal of Educational Psychology* **65**, 113–24.

Riding, R. J. and Cheema, I. (1991) 'Cognitive Styles – an overview and integration', *Educational Psychology* **11**, 193–215.

Riding, R. J. and Calvey, I. (1981) 'The assessment of verbal–imagery learning styles and their effect on the recall of concrete and abstract prose passages by eleven year old children', *British Journal of Psychology* **72**, 59–64.

Riding, R. J. and Craig, O. (1998) 'Cognitive style and problem behaviour in boys referred to residential special schools', *Educational Studies* **24**, 205–22.

Riding, R. J. and Craig, O. (1999) 'Cognitive style and types of problem behaviour in boys special schools', *British Journal of Educational Psychology* **69**, 307–22.

Riding, R. J., Dahraei, H., Grimley, M. and Banner, G. (2001) *Working Memory, Cognitive Style and Academic Attainment* (submitted for publication).

Riding, R. J. and Douglas, G. (1993) 'The effect of cognitive style and mode of presentation on learning performance', *British Journal of Educational Psychology* **63**, 297–307.

Riding R. J. and Dyer, V. A. (1980) 'The relationship between extraversion and verbal–imagery learning style in twelve year old children', *Personality and Individual Differences* **1**, 273–9.

Riding, R. J. and Fairhurst, P. (2001) 'Cognitive style, home background and conduct behaviour in primary school pupils', *Educational Psychology* **21**, 115–24.

Riding, R. J. and Grimley, M. (1999) 'Cognitive style and learning from multimedia materials in 11-year-old children', *British Journal of Educational Technology* **30**, 45–56.

Riding, R. J. and Grimley, M. (2001) 'Cognitive style, gender and learning in 11-year-old children' (submitted for publication).

Riding, R. J., Grimley, M., Dahraei, H. and Banner, G. (2001) 'Cognitive style, working memory and learning behaviour and attainment in school subjects' (submitted for publication).

Riding, R. J. and Mathias, D. (1991) 'Cognitive styles and preferred learning mode, reading attainment and cognitive ability in 11-year-old children', *Educational Psychology* **11**, 383–93.

Riding, R. J. and Pearson, F. (1994) 'The relationship between cognitive style and intelligence', *Educational Psychology* **14**, 413–25.

Riding, R. J. and Rayner, S. (1998) *Cognitive Styles and Learning Strategies.* London: David Fulton Publishers.

Riding, R. J. and Read, G. (1996) 'Cognitive style and pupil learning preferences', *Educational Psychology* **16**, 81–106.

Riding, R. J. and Sadler-Smith, E. (1992) 'Type of instructional material, cognitive style and learning performance', *Educational Studies* **18**, 323–40.

Riding, R. J. and Sadler-Smith, E. (1997) 'Cognitive style and learning strategies: Some implications for training design', *International Journal of Training and Development* **1**, 199–208.

Riding, R. J. and Staley, A. (1998) 'Self-perception as learner, cognitive style and business studies students' course performance', *Assessment and Evaluation in Higher Education* **23**, 43–58.

Riding, R. J. and Taylor, E. M. (1976) 'Imagery performance and prose comprehension in seven-year-old children', *Educational Studies* **2**, 21–7.

Riding, R. J. and Watts, M. (1997) 'The effect of cognitive style on the preferred format of instructional material', *Educational Psychology* **17**, 179–83.

Riding, R. J. and Wigley, S. (1997) 'The relationship between cognitive style and personality in further education students', *Personality and Individual Differences* **23**, 379–89.

Riley, D. and Shaw, M. (1985) *Parental Supervision and Juvenile Delinquency*. London: HMSO.

Rumberger, R., Ghatak, R., Poulos, G., Ritter, P. and Dornbusch, S. (1990) 'Family influences in dropout behavior in one California high school', *Sociology of Education* **63**, 83–99.

Rutter, M., Maughan, B., Mortimore, P. and Ouston, J. (1979) *Fifteen Thousand Hours: Secondary Schools and their Effects on Children*. London: Open Books.

Sadler-Smith, E. and Riding, R. J. (1999) 'Cognitive style and instructional preferences', *Instructional Science* **27**, 355–71.

Schwartzman, A. E., Varlaan, P., Peters, P. and Serbin, L. A. (1995) 'Sex roles in coercion', in J. McCord (ed.) *Coercion and Punishment in Long-Term Perspectives*. Cambridge: Cambridge University Press.

Shah, P. and Miyake, A. (1996) 'The separability of working memory resources for spatial thinking and language processing: An individual differences approach', *Journal of Experimental Psychology: General* **125**, 4–27.

Sones, A. M. and Stroud, J. B. (1940) 'Review with special reference to temporal position', *Journal of Educational Psychology* **31**, 665–76.

Spielberger, C. D. (1977) *State and Trait Anxiety Inventory Form Y-1*. Palo Alto: Consulting Psychologists Press.

Spitzer, H. F. (1939) 'Studies in retention', *Journal of Educational Psychology* **30**, 641–56.

Tulving, E. and Craik, F. I. M. (eds) (1999) *The Oxford Handbook of Memory*. New York: Oxford University Press.

Turner, M. L. and Engle, R. W. (1989) 'Is working memory capacity task dependent', *Journal of Memory and Language* **28**, 127–54.

Wilson, H. (1980) 'Parental supervision: A neglected aspect of delinquency', *British Journal of Criminology* **20**, 203–35.

Winkley, L. (1996) *Emotional Problems in Children and Young People*. London: Cassell.

Zimiles, H. and Lee, V. (1991) 'Adolescent family structure and educational progress', *Developmental Psychology* **27**, 314–20.

Author index

Subject index